# GC_E

# **M**athematics

## Intermediate

**Author**
Fiona C Mapp

**Series editor**
Alan Brewerton

## *Letts*
### EDUCATIONAL

**Revision Notes**

Every effort has been made to trace copyright holders and to obtain their permission for the use of copyright material. The authors and publishers will gladly receive information enabling them to rectify any error or omission in subsequent editions.

First published 1997
Reprinted 1997, 1998
New edition 1998

Letts Educational, Schools and Colleges Division
9–15 Aldine Street, London W12 8AW
Tel.  0181 740 2270
Fax. 0181 740 2280

Text © Fiona C Mapp 1998

Editorial, design and production by Hart McLeod, Cambridge

**British Library Cataloguing-in-Publication Data**
A CIP record for this book is available from the British Library

ISBN 1 85758 135 X

Printed and bound in Great Britain

Letts Educational is the trading name of BPP (Letts Educational) Ltd

**Acknowledgements**
The author and publisher are grateful to the staff at Cottenham Village College, Cambridge, for their technical assistance.

# Contents

# Introduction

This book has been specifically designed to help you prepare for your GCSE exams in the easiest and most effective way. Keep this book with you throughout your revision – it is the key to your success.

## How to use this book

All the information you need to know for your course is presented as a series of brief facts and explanations. These will help you understand and remember your work. Each page has a margin containing key tips from examiners showing you how to get extra marks or how to avoid common mistakes. There is also plenty of space in the margin for you to highlight key points, write your own notes and make references to other materials (class notes, textbooks, etc.). This will help you decide in which topics you feel confident or areas you do not fully understand. There is a short test at the end of each topic which will help test your understanding and boost your memory.

## Preparing your revision programme

In most subjects you will have coursework, homework, revision, practice examination questions and a final examination. The examination may cause you the most anxiety. With proper preparation, however, you do not need to worry.

Make sure that you have allowed enough time to revise your work and make a list of all the things you have to do and your coursework deadlines.

## Most important of all ... GOOD LUCK!

# The examiner's report

Every year the examination boards publish reports on the previous year's examinations. The reports show areas in the examinations where students have performed well or badly and highlights mistakes that students frequently make. The examiners' reports can help you avoid making mistakes and therefore gain extra marks. **Recent examiners' reports highlight the following areas where students lost marks.**

- Lack of appropriate equipment, for example protractors, compasses and rulers.

- Insufficient or confused working out. In questions requiring calculations answers were often rounded off too quickly or not given to the required accuracy, e.g. 2 d.p. or 3 s.f., etc.

- Lack of correct units, particularly in questions where you are told to state your units.

- Vague answers with little reference to the data when answering questions which ask you to 'Explain'.

- Lack of knowledge of metric and imperial conversions.

- Inability to use your calculators efficiently, particularly in topics of standard form, substitution of formulae, trigonometry and powers.

- Poor skills in algebraic manipulation, e.g. the ability to solve equations and inequalities.

# Common areas of difficulty

**Some common areas of difficulty on Intermediate Level examination papers have occurred in the following topics:**

- Standard index form   page 12

- Percentage increase or decrease   page 21

- Reverse percentage problems   page 21

- Compound interest   page 26

- Drawing and interpretation of graphs   pages 32–36

- Brackets, factorisation and rearranging formulae   pages 39–41

- Solving simultaneous and quadratic equations   pages 42–44

- Inequalities   pages 44–45

- The application of Pythagoras' theorem and trigonometry to problems   page 53

- Transformations   pages 58–61

- Similarity   pages 61–62

- Locus   pages 64–65

- Dimensions   page 72

- Averages of grouped data   page 81

- Using averages to compare distributions   page 83

- Relative frequency   pages 86–87

- Tree diagrams   pages 88–89

# Number and algebra

## Place value and the number system

### Integers

Examiner's tips and your notes

The integers are the set of numbers {. . ., –3, –2, –1, 0, 1, 2, 3, . . .}.

When referring to integers, the term **integral value** is used. A number that is **non-integral** is not an integer.

## Directed numbers

These are numbers which may be **positive** or **negative**. Positive are above zero, negative are below zero.

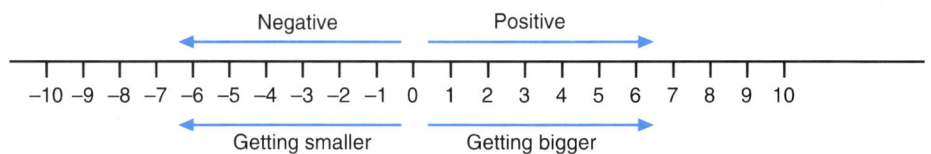

### Examples

–10 is smaller than –8.    –10 < –8

–4 is bigger than –8.      –4 > –8

2 is bigger than –6.       2 > –6

### Adding and subtracting directed numbers

#### Example
The temperature at 6 a.m. was –5 °C. By 10 a.m. it had risen 8 degrees. So the new temperature was 3 °C.

Draw a number line if it helps.

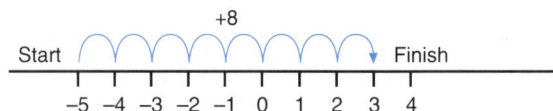

#### Example
Find the value of –2 – 4.

$$-2 - 4$$

Note the different uses of the minus sign.

This represents the **sign** of the number. Start at –2.

This represents the operation of **subtraction**. Move 4 places to the left.

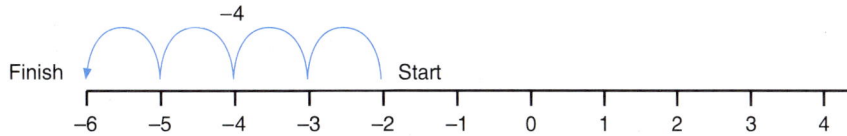

So $-2 - 4 = -6$

When the number to be added (or subtracted) is **negative**, the normal direction of movement is **reversed**.

**Example**

$$-4 - (-3) \quad \text{is the same as} \quad -4 + 3 = -1$$

The negative changes the direction.

Move 3 places to the right.

When two (+) or two (−) signs are together, these rules are used:

$$\left. \begin{array}{l} +(+) \to + \\ -(-) \to + \end{array} \right\} \text{like signs give a positive,} \qquad \left. \begin{array}{l} +(-) \to - \\ -(+) \to - \end{array} \right\} \text{unlike signs give a negative.}$$

**Examples**

$$-6 + (-2) = -6 - 2 = -8 \qquad -2 - (+6) = -2 - 6 = -8$$
$$4 - (-3) = 4 + 3 = 7 \qquad 9 + (-3) = 9 - 3 = 6$$

## Multiplying and dividing directed numbers

Multiply and divide the numbers as normal. Then find the sign for the answer using these rules:

• two **like** signs (both + or both −) give **positive**,

• two **unlike** signs (one + and the other −) give **negative**.

**Examples**
$$-6 \times (+4) = -24 \qquad -12 \div (-3) = 4$$
$$-6 \times (-3) = 18 \qquad 20 \div (-4) = -5$$

## Negative numbers on the calculator

Use a calculator when working with negative numbers (if possible).

The $\boxed{+/-}$ or $\boxed{(-)}$ key on the calculator gives a negative number.

For example, to get −6, press $\boxed{6}$ $\boxed{+/-}$ or $\boxed{(-)}$ $\boxed{6}$.

This represents the sign.

7

**Example**

$$-4 - (-2) = -2$$

is keyed in the calculator like this:

4 [+/-] [−] 2 [+/-] [=]

*sign*       *operation*   *sign*

> Make sure you know how to enter it in **your** calculator.

# Fractions

A fraction is a part of a whole one. $\frac{4}{5}$ means 4 parts out of 5.

The top number is the **numerator**. The bottom one is the **denominator**.

A fraction like $\frac{4}{5}$ is called a **proper fraction**.

A fraction like $\frac{24}{17}$ is called an **improper fraction**.

# Using the fraction key on the calculator

[aᵇ/c] is the fraction key on the calculator.

**Example**

$\frac{12}{18}$ is keyed in as 1 2 [aᵇ/c] 1 8.

This is displayed as [ 12⌐18 ] or [ 12⊢18 ].

The calculator will automatically cancel down fractions when the [=] key is pressed. For example, $\frac{12}{18}$ becomes [ 2⌐3 ] or [ 2⊢3 ].

> This means two-thirds.

Check: your calculator may have a [2nd] or [inv] key instead of [shift].

A display of [ 1⌐4⌐9 ] means $1\frac{4}{9}$. If you now press [shift] [aᵇ/c], it converts back to an improper fraction, [ 13⌐9 ].

# Decimals

A decimal point is used to separate whole-number columns from fractional columns.

**Example**

| Thousands | Hundreds | Tens | Units | Tenths | Hundredths | Thousandths |
|-----------|----------|------|-------|--------|------------|-------------|
| 5 | 9 | 2 | 4 • | 1 | 6 | 3 |

*decimal point*

- The 1 means $\frac{1}{10}$.

- The 6 means $\frac{6}{100}$.

- The 3 means $\frac{3}{1000}$.

> Remember, hundredths are smaller than tenths.
>
> $\frac{10}{100} = \frac{1}{10}$ so $\frac{6}{100} < \frac{1}{10}$

## Recurring decimals

A decimal that **recurs** is shown by placing a dot over the numbers that repeat.

**Examples**

$$0.333\ldots = 0.\dot{3}$$

$$0.17777\ldots = 0.1\dot{7}$$

$$0.232323\ldots = 0.\dot{2}\dot{3}$$

## Ordering decimals

When ordering decimals:

- first write them with the same number of figures after the decimal point;

- then compare whole numbers, digits in the tenths place, digits in the hundredths place, and so on.

**Example**

Arrange these numbers in order of size, smallest first:

6.21, 6.023, 6.4, 6.04, 2.71, 9.4

First rewrite them:

6.210, 6.023, 6.400, 6.040, 2.710, 9.400

Then re-order them:

2.710, 6.023, 6.040, 6.210, 6.400, 9.400

> Always check that all values have been included.

# Rounding numbers

## Decimal places (d.p.)

When rounding numbers to a specified number of decimal places:

- look at the last number that is wanted (if rounding 12.367 to 2 d.p., look at the 6 (second d.p.));

- look at the number next to it (look at the number not needed – the 7);

- if it is **5 or more**, then **round up** the last digit (7 is greater than 5, so round the 6 up to a 7);

- if it is **less than 5**, the digit remains the **same**.

## Examples

Round 12.49 to 1 d.p.

12.4**9** rounds up to 12.5.

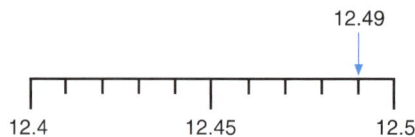

Round 8.735 to 2 d.p.

8.73**5** rounds up to 8.74.

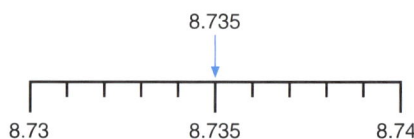

Round 9.624 to 2 d.p.

9.62**4** rounds to 9.62.

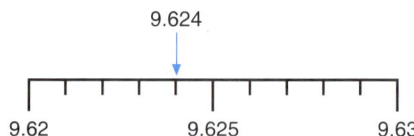

# Significant figures (s.f. or sig. fig.)

Apply the same rule as with decimal places: if the next digit is 5 or more, round up.

The 1st significant figure is the first digit which is not a zero. The 2nd, 3rd, 4th, . . . significant figures follow on after the 1st digit. They may or may not be zeros.

## Examples

6.4027 has 5 s.f.

1st 2nd 3rd 4th 5th

0.000 470 1 has 4 s.f.

1st 2nd 3rd 4th

*Take care when rounding that you do not change the place values.*

## Examples

| Number | to 3 s.f. | to 2 s.f. | to 1 s.f. |
|---|---|---|---|
| 4.207 | 4.21 | 4.2 | 4 |
| 4379 | 4380 | 4400 | 4000 |
| 0.006 209 | 0.006 21 | 0.0062 | 0.006 |

After rounding the last digit, you must fill in the end zeros. For example, 4380 = 4400 to 2 s.f. (not 44).

# Percentages

These are fractions with a denominator of 100. For example $75\% = \frac{75}{100}$.

# Ratios

A ratio is used to **compare** two or more related quantities.

A colon : is used to mean 'compared to'. For example, '16 boys compared to 20 girls' is written as '16:20'.

To **simplify** ratios, use the calculator fraction key.

## Examples

The ratio 16:20 can be keyed in as ⊡1⊡ ⊡6⊡ ⊡aᵇ/c⊡ ⊡2⊡ ⊡0⊡ ⊡=⊡ ⊡4⌐5⊡ = 4:5

The ratio 20:16 can be keyed in as ⊡2⊡ ⊡0⊡ ⊡aᵇ/c⊡ ⊡1⊡ ⊡6⊡ ⊡=⊡ ⊡5⌐4⊡ = 5:4

Ratios can also be simplified by cancelling factors. 16:20 = 4:5 (divide both sides by 4).

shift aᵇ/c
changes this back to an improper fraction on some calculators.

# Equivalences between fractions, decimals and percentages

Fractions, decimals and percentages all mean the same thing but are just written in a different way.

| Fraction | | Decimal | | Percentage |
|---|---|---|---|---|
| $\frac{1}{2}$ | $1 \div 2 \rightarrow$ | 0.5 | $\times 100\% \rightarrow$ | 50% |
| $\frac{3}{5}$ | | 0.6 | | 60% |
| $\frac{1}{3}$ | | $0.3\dot{3}$ | | $33.\dot{3}\%$ |

## Ordering different numbers

When putting fractions, decimals and percentages in order of size, it is best to change them all to **decimals** first.

## Example

Place in order of size, smallest first:

$\frac{3}{5}$, 0.65, 0.273, 27%, 62%, $\frac{4}{9}$

0.6, 0.65, 0.273, 0.27, 0.62, $0.4\dot{4}$        Put into decimals first.

0.27, 0.273, $0.\dot{4}4$, 0.6, 0.62, 0.65        Now order.

27%, 0.273, $\frac{4}{9}$, $\frac{3}{5}$, 62%, 0.65        Now rewrite them back in their original form.

Make sure you put the values in the order the question says.

# Indices

An **index** is sometimes known as a **power**.

## Examples

$6^4$ is read as **6 to the power 4**. It means $6 \times 6 \times 6 \times 6$.

$2^7$ is read as **2 to the power 7**. It means $2 \times 2 \times 2 \times 2 \times 2 \times 2 \times 2$.

$a^b$    the **index** or **power**

the **base**

The **base** has to be the **same** when the rules of indices are applied.

## Rules of indices

You need to learn these rules:

- When **multiplying, add** the powers.

  $4^7 \times 4^3 = 4^{7+3} = 4^{10}$

- When **dividing, subtract** the powers.

  $6^9 \div 6^4 = 6^{9-4} = 6^5$

- When **raising one power to another, multiply** the powers.

  $(7^2)^4 = 7^{2 \times 4} = 7^8$

- Anything raised to the **power zero** is just **1**, provided the number is not zero.

  $5^0 = 1$        $6^0 = 1$

  $2.7189^0 = 1$     $0^0 =$ undefined

- Anything to the **power 1** is just **itself**.

  $15^1 = 15$       $1923^1 = 1923$

The above rules also apply when the powers are negative.

### Examples

$6^{-2} \times 6^{12} = 6^{-2+12} = 6^{10}$

$8^{-4} \times 8^{-3} = 8^{-4+-3} = 8^{-7}$

$(6^4)^{-2} = 6^{4 \times -2} = 6^{-8}$

## Standard index form (or standard form)

Standard index form is used to write very large numbers or very small numbers in a simpler way. When written in standard form the number will be written as:

Standard form questions are very common at GCSE.

$a \times 10^n$

**a** must be between 1 and 10, $1 \le a < 10$.

The value of $n$ is the number of times the decimal point has to move to the right to return the number to its original value.

### Big numbers

### Examples

Write 6 230 000 in standard form.

- Move the decimal point to between the 6 and 2 to give 6.230000 ($1 \le 6.23 < 10$).

- Count how many places the decimal point needs to be moved to restore the number.

  6 2 3 0 0 0 0 (6 places)

- In standard form 6 230 000 = $6.23 \times 10^6$

4371 = $4.371 \times 10^3$ in standard form

## Small numbers

### Examples

Write 0.003 71 in standard form.

- Move the decimal point to between the 3 and 7 to give 3.71 ($1 \leq 3.71 < 10$).

- Count how many places the decimal point has been moved.

0.003 71　　(3 places)

- In standard form $0.003\ 71 = 3.71 \times 10^{-3}$

$0.000\ 047\ 9 = 4.79 \times 10^{-5}$ in standard form.

*This means that the decimal point is moved 3 places to the **left**.*

## Standard form and the calculator

*The* EXP *key has the effect of putting the × 10 part in for you!*

To key a number in standard form into the calculator, use the EXP key. (Some calculators use EE . Make sure that you check your calculator.)

### Examples

$6.23 \times 10^6$ is keyed in as: 6 · 2 3 EXP 6

$4.93 \times 10^{-5}$ is keyed in as: 4 · 9 3 EXP 5 +/−

Most calculators do not show standard form correctly on the display.

7.632 09 means $7.632 \times 10^9$.

4.62 −07 means $4.62 \times 10^{-7}$.

*You will lose lots of marks if you miss out the ×10 part.*

Remember to put in the × 10 part if it has been left out.

## Calculations with standard form

Use the calculator to do complex calculations in standard form.

### Examples

$(2.6 \times 10^3) \times (8.9 \times 10^{12}) = 2.314 \times 10^{16}$

This would be keyed in as:

2 · 6 EXP 3 x 8 · 9 EXP 1 2 =

*Check that it can be done on your calculator.*

Check that for $(1.8 \times 10^6) \div (2.7 \times 10^{-3})$ the answer is $6.\dot{6} \times 10^8$

Just key in as normal: 2 · 7 EXP 3 +/−

# Questions

1 If the temperature was −12 °C at 2 a.m. and it rose by 15 degrees by 11 a.m., what was the temperature at 11 a.m?

2 Work these out without a calculator.

(a) −2 − (−6) =  (b) −9 + (−7) =  (c) −2 × 6 =

(d) −9 + (−3) =  (e) −20 ÷ (−4) =  (f) −18 ÷ (−3) =

3 Round the following numbers to 2 decimal places (2 d.p.).

(a) 6.249  (b) 18.071  (c) 106.2794

(d) 3.755  (e) 27.0629  (f) 18.0935

4 Round the following numbers to 3 significant figures (3 s.f.).

(a) 0.003 786  (b) 27 490  (c) 307 250

5 Change the fraction $\frac{12}{18}$ into a decimal and percentage.

6 Place these values in order, putting the smallest first.

61%,  94%,  0.93,  $\frac{9}{10}$,  $\frac{4}{7}$,  0.274

7 Simplify these.

(a) $12^4 \times 12^8$  (b) $9^{-2} \times 9^{-4}$  (c) $4^0$

(d) $18^6 \div 18^{-2}$  (e) $(4^2)^5$  (f) $1^{20}$

8 Write these numbers in standard index form.

(a) 694 000 000  (b) 0.003 729

(c) 2790  (d) 0.027

9 Work these out on a calculator. Give your answers to 3 s.f.

(a) $\dfrac{1.279 \times 10^9}{2.94 \times 10^{-2}}$  (b) $(1.693 \times 10^4) \times (2.71 \times 10^{12})$

10 Complete the table.

| Fraction | Decimal | Percentage |
|----------|---------|------------|
|          |         | 75%        |
| $\frac{2}{5}$ |    |            |
|          | $0.\dot{3}$ |        |

# Relationships between numbers and computation methods

## Using a calculator

Examiner's tips and your notes

## Important calculator keys

Practise using your own calculator. Make sure you know where these keys are.

(−) or +/− These change positive numbers to negative ones.

C This only cancels the last key you have pressed.

AC This cancels all the work.

If possible, use the C key as it saves lots of time.

$a^{b/c}$ This key allows a fraction to be put in the calculator.

Shift or 2nd or Inv These allow 2nd functions to be carried out.

$y^x$ or $x^y$ These work out powers.

Min, MR, M+ These are memory keys.

[(...., ....)] These are brackets keys.

When calculating complex fractions, use either the bracket keys or the memory keys.

### Example

$$\frac{15 \times 10 + 46}{9.3 \times 2.1} = 10.04 \text{ (2 d.p.)}$$

Make sure you understand how **your** calculator works.

This may be keyed in as:

[(.... 15 × 10 + 46 ....)] ÷ [(.... 9.3 × 2.1 ....)] =

The above could be as easily done using the memory keys. Try writing down the key sequence for yourself.

## Calculating powers

Make sure you know how to use the power key as it saves lots of time.

$y^x$ or $x^y$ is used for calculating powers such as $2^7$.

- Use the power key on the calculator to work out $2^7$.

- Write down calculator keys used.

- Check that you obtain the answer 128.

Now try writing down the keys that would be needed for these calculations. Check that you get the right answers.

(a) $\dfrac{2.9 \times 3.6}{(4.2 + 3.7)} = 1.322$  (b) $9^{1/3} \times 4^5 = 2130$  (c) $\dfrac{3 \times (5.2)^2}{9.6 \times (12.4)^3} = 4.432 \times 10^{-3}$

# Types of number

## Multiples

These are just the numbers in multiplication tables.
For example, multiples of 8 are 8, 16, 24, 32, 40,. . .

## Factors

These are whole numbers which **divide exactly** into another number. For example, the factors of 20 are 1, 2, 4, 5, 10, 20.

Factors of 20 can be split up into factor pairs.

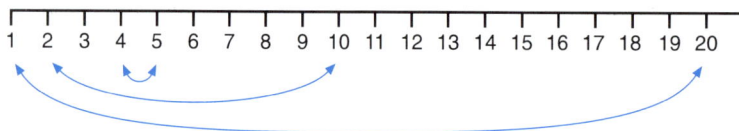

To find all the factors of a number, start at 1 and divide by each number in turn.

```
1   2   3   4   5   6   7   8   9   10  11  12  13  14  15  16  17  18  19  20
```

So 1 × 20 = 20

2 × 10 = 20

4 × 5 = 20

## Prime numbers

These are numbers which only have two factors, **1 and itself**. Note that 1 is **not** a prime number. The smallest prime number is 2, which is also the only even prime number.

Make sure you know the prime numbers up to 20.

Prime numbers up to 20 are 2, 3, 5, 7, 11, 13, 17, 19.

## Prime factors

These are factors which are prime.

Some numbers can be written as a product of its prime factors.

**Example**

The diagram shows the prime factors of 360.

- Divide 360 by its first prime factor, 2.
- Divide 180 by its first prime factor, 2.
- Keep on going until the final number is prime.

As a product of its prime factors 360 may be written as:

2 × 2 × 2 × 3 × 3 × 5 = 360

or $2^3 \times 3^2 \times 5 = 360$

in **index** notation (using powers).

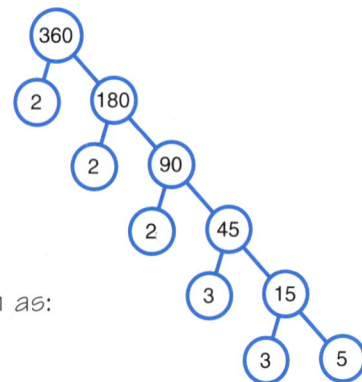

## Highest common factor (HCF)

The **largest factor** that two numbers have in common is called the **HCF**.

**Example**

Find the HCF of 84 and 360.

- Write the numbers as products of their prime factors.

$$84 \ = 2 \times 2 \quad \times 3 \quad \times 7$$
$$360 = 2 \times 2 \times 2 \times 3 \times 3 \times 5$$

- Ring the factors in common.

- These give the HCF = 2 × 2 × 3 = 12.

## Lowest common multiple (LCM)

This is the **lowest** number which is a **multiple** of two numbers.

**Example**

Find the LCM of 6 and 8.

$$8 = 2 \times 2 \times 2$$
$$6 = \qquad 2 \times 3$$

8 and 6 have a common prime factor of 2. So it is only counted once.

The LCM of 6 and 8 is 2 × 2 × 2 × 3 = 24.

## Squares and cubes

Anything to the **power 2** is **square**. For example, $6^2 = 6 \times 6 = 36$ (six squared).

Anything to the **power 3** is **cube**. For example, $5^3 = 5 \times 5 \times 5 = 125$ (five cubed).

Square numbers include:

1,     4,     9,     16,     25,     36,     49,     64, 81, 100,. . .
(1 × 1), (2 × 2), (3 × 3), (4 × 4), (5 × 5), (6 × 6), (7 × 7), . . .

Cube numbers include:

1,         8,         27,     64, 125,. . .
(1 × 1 × 1), (2 × 2 × 2), (3 × 3 × 3), . . .

It is important that you can recognise square and cube numbers.

## Square roots and cube roots

$\sqrt{\phantom{x}}$ is the **square root sign**. Taking the square root is the opposite of squaring. For example, $\sqrt{25} = 5$ since $5^2 = 25$.

$\sqrt[3]{\phantom{x}}$ is the **cube root sign**. Taking the cube root is the opposite of cubing. For example, $\sqrt[3]{8} = 2$ since $2^3 = 8$.

## Reciprocals

The reciprocal of a number $\frac{a}{x}$ is $\frac{x}{a}$ $(= x \div a)$.

**Examples**

The reciprocal of $\frac{2}{3}$ is $\frac{3}{2}$.

The reciprocal of 4 is $\frac{1}{4}$ because 4 is the same as $\frac{4}{1}$.

To find the reciprocal of $1\frac{2}{3}$, first put it in the form $\frac{a}{x}$ (so $1\frac{2}{3} = \frac{5}{3}$), and then invert it ($\frac{3}{5}$).

# Multiplying and dividing by numbers between 0 and 1

When **multiplying** by numbers between 0 and 1, the result is **smaller** than the starting value.

When **dividing** by numbers between 0 and 1, the result is **bigger** than the starting value.

**Examples**

$6 \times 0.1 = 0.6$

$6 \times 0.01 = 0.06$

$6 \times 0.001 = 0.006$

The result is **smaller** than the starting value.

$6 \div 0.1 = 60$

$6 \div 0.01 = 600$

$6 \div 0.001 = 6000$

The result is **bigger** than the starting value.

# Fractions

When the numerator is **less than** the denominator, it is a **proper fraction**, e.g. $\frac{4}{5}$.

When the numerator is **bigger than** the denominator, it is an **improper fraction**, e.g. $\frac{5}{4}$.

$2\frac{1}{2}$ is called a **mixed number**.

## Addition and subtraction of fractions

These examples show the basic principles of adding and subtracting fractions.

**Example**

$\frac{1}{8} + \frac{3}{4}$ • First make the denominators the same: $\frac{3}{4} = \frac{6}{8}$

$\frac{3}{4}$ is **equivalent** to $\frac{6}{8}$.

$= \frac{1}{8} + \frac{6}{8}$ • Replace $\frac{3}{4}$ with $\frac{6}{8}$ so that the denominators are the same.

$= \frac{7}{8}$ • Add the numerators $1 + 6 = 7$. **Do not add** the denominators; the denominator stays the same number.

**Example**

$\frac{9}{12} - \frac{1}{3}$ • First make the denominators the same: $\frac{1}{3} = \frac{4}{12}$

$\frac{1}{3}$ is equivalent to $\frac{4}{12}$.

$= \frac{9}{12} - \frac{4}{12}$ • Replace the $\frac{1}{3}$ with $\frac{4}{12}$.

$= \frac{5}{12}$ • Subtract the numerators but **not** the denominators; the denominator stays the same number.

If you have a fraction key on your calculator, use it to check.

On the calculator key in.

9 $\boxed{a^b/_c}$ 12 $\boxed{-}$ 1 $\boxed{a^b/_c}$ 3 $\boxed{=}$

## Multiplication and division of fractions

When multiplying and dividing fractions, write out whole or mixed numbers as improper fractions before starting.

**Example**

$\frac{2}{9} \times \frac{4}{7} = \frac{2 \times 4}{9 \times 7} = \frac{8}{63}$ ◄——— Multiply numerators together.
◄——— Multiply denominators together.

Change a division into a multiplication by turning the second fraction upside down and multiplying both fractions together; that is, **multiply by the reciprocal.**

**Example**

$\frac{7}{9} \div \frac{12}{18} = \frac{7}{9} \times \frac{18}{12}$ Take the **reciprocal** of the **second fraction**.

$= \frac{126}{108} = 1\frac{1}{6}$ Rewrite the answer as a mixed number.

# Percentages

## Percentage of a quantity

The word '**of**' means **multiply**. For example, 40% of £600 becomes
$\frac{40}{100} \times 600 = £240$

On the calculator key in

40 $\boxed{\div}$ 100 $\boxed{\times}$ 600 $\boxed{=}$

Questions involving percentages appear on the exam paper every year and so it is important to be aware of the various techniques required.

## One quantity as a percentage of another

To make the answer a **percentage**, multiply **by 100%**.

### Example
In a carton of milk, 6.2 g of the contents are fat. If 2.5 g of the fat is saturated, what percentage is this?

$$\frac{2.5}{6.2} \times 100\% = 40.3\% \text{ (to 1 d.p.)}$$

*Multiply by 100% to get a percentage.*

On the calculator key in

2.5 ÷ 6.2 × 100 =

# Proportional changes with fractions and percentages

## Increase and decrease

There are two methods. Use the one that is familiar.

### Example
Last year there were 290 people who belong to a Gym. This year there are $\frac{3}{5}$ more. How many people now belong?

### Method 1
$\frac{3}{5} \times 290 = 174$      Work out $\frac{3}{5}$ of 290.

$290 + 174 = 464$ people      Add this on to the original number.

*Always check that you have answered the question.*

### Method 2
Increasing by $\frac{3}{5}$ is the same as multiplying by $1\frac{3}{5}$ $(1 + \frac{3}{5})$.

$1\frac{3}{5} \times 290 = 464$

On the calculator key in

1 $a^{b/c}$ 3 $a^{b/c}$ 5 × 290 =

*Use the fraction key to work this out, if possible.*

### Example
A three-piece suite costing £1300 is reduced in a sale by 35%. What is the sale price of the suite?

### Method 1
$\frac{35}{100} \times £1300 = £455$

New price = £1300 − £455 = £845

## Method 2

Decreasing by 35% is the same as finding 100% − 35% = 65% of the original cost.

65% = 0.65 which is the **scale factor**.

0.65 × £1300 = £845

*As the scale factor is less than 1, it reduces the value.*

# Repeated percentage change

## Example

*Work these questions out year by year.*

A car was bought for £8000 in 1994. Each year it depreciates in value by 20%. What is the car worth 3 years later?

- Find 80% of the value of the car first.

  Year 1    $\frac{80}{100}$ × £8000 = £6400

*Beware: do not do 3 × 20 = 60% reduction over 3 years!*

- Then work out the value year by year.

  Year 2    $\frac{80}{100}$ × £6400 = £5120 (£6400 depreciates in value by 20%.)

  Year 3    $\frac{80}{100}$ × £5120 = £4096 after 3 years (£5120 depreciates by 20%.)

# Percentage increase or decrease

The answer will be a percentage so multiply by 100%.

$$\% \text{ change} = \frac{change}{original} \times 100\%$$

## Example

A coat costs £125. In a sale it is reduced to £85. What is the percentage reduction?

Reduction = £125 − £85 = £40

$\frac{40}{125}$ × 100% = 32%

*Remember to divide by the original value.*

# Reverse percentage problems

This is when the **original quantity** is calculated.

## Example

*Always read these questions very carefully.*

The price of a television is reduced by 20% in the sales. It **now** costs £250. What was the original price?

- The sale price is 100% − 20% = 80% of the pre-sale price.

$\frac{80}{100} = 0.8$

$0.8 \times \text{(price)} = £250$

$\text{price} = \frac{250}{0.8} = £312.50$

It is 80% of the original price which is being found, not 80% of the new price.

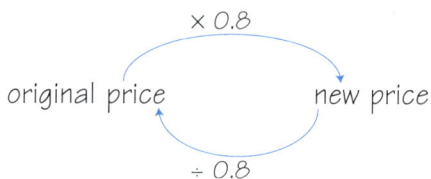

original price → new price

× 0.8

÷ 0.8

Using a diagram in the exam may help you to understand the problem and clarify the process.

- Always check the answer is sensible.
- Is the original price more than the sale price?

# Ratio calculations

## Sharing a quantity in a given ratio

- Add up the total parts.
- Work out what one part is worth.
- Work out what the other parts are worth.

### Example

£20 000 is shared in the ratio 1 : 4 between Ewan and Leroy. How much does each receive?

$1 + 4 = 5 \text{ parts}$

$5 \text{ parts} = £20\ 000$

$1 \text{ part} = \frac{£20\ 000}{5} = £4000$

So Ewan gets $1 \times £4000 = £4000$ and Leroy gets $4 \times £4000 = £16\ 000$.

Check by adding the amount of money each receives. This should equal the amount of money shared out.

## Increasing and decreasing in a given ratio

- Divide to get one part.
- Multiply for each new part.

### Example

A photograph of length 9 cm is to be enlarged in the ratio 5 : 3. What is the length of the enlarged photograph?

- Divide 9 cm by 3 to get 1 part.

  $9 \div 3 = 3$

- Multiply this by 5. So $5 \times 3 = 15$ cm on the enlarged photograph.

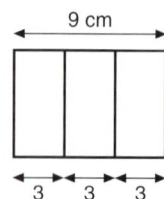

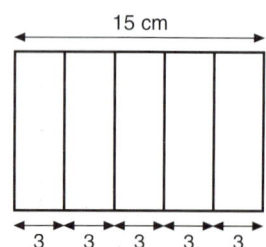

9 cm

3   3   3

15 cm

3   3   3   3   3

### Example

A recipe uses 1400 g of flour for 4 people. How much is needed for 6 people?

### Method 1

- Divide 1400g by 4, 350 g for 1 person.
- Multiply this by 6. So 350 g × 6 = 2100 g for 6 people.

### Method 2

$4 : 6 \rightarrow 2 : 3 \rightarrow 1 : 1.5$

So 1400 g × 1.5 = 2100 g for 6 people.

*1.5 is the scale factor.*

# Estimates and approximations

Estimating is a good way of checking answers.

- Round the numbers to 'easy' numbers, usually 1 or 2 significant figures.
- Work out the estimate using these easy numbers.
- Use the symbol ≈, which means '**approximately equal to**'.

For multiplying or dividing, never approximate a number with zero. Use 0.1, 0.01, 0.001, etc.

### Examples

(a)  $8.93 \times 25.09 \approx 10 \times 25 = 250$

(b)  $(6.29)^2 \approx 6^2 = 36$

(c)  $\dfrac{296 \times 52.1}{9.72 \times 1.14} \approx \dfrac{300 \times 50}{10 \times 1} = \dfrac{15\,000}{10} = 1500$

(d)  $0.096 \times 79.2 \approx 0.1 \times 80 = 8$

*To obtain full marks you must show all of your working out.*

### Example

Jack does the calculation $\dfrac{9.6 \times 103}{(2.9)^2}$.

(a) Estimate the answer to this calculation, without using a calculator.

(b) Jack's answer is 1175.7. Is this the right order of magnitude?

(a)  Estimate: $\dfrac{9.6 \times 103}{(2.9)^2} \approx \dfrac{10 \times 100}{3^2} = \dfrac{1000}{9} \approx \dfrac{1000}{10} = 100$

(b)  Jack's answer is not the right order of magnitude. It is ten times too big.

*Right order of magnitude means 'about the right size'.*

When adding and subtracting, very small numbers may be approximated to zero.

### Examples

$109.6 + 0.0002 \approx 110 + 0 = 110$

$63.87 - 0.01 \approx 64 - 0 = 64$

# Questions

1  List the prime numbers up to 20.

2  Find the HCF and LCM of 24 and 60.

3  Find   (a) $\sqrt{64}$   (b) $\sqrt[3]{216}$

4  Write down the reciprocals of:  (a) $\frac{9}{12}$  (b) $\frac{x}{p}$

5  Without using a calculator, work out these.

   (a)  $2.62 \times 1000$   (b)  $600 \times 400$   (c)  $12.4 \times 100$

   (d)  $8 \times 0.001$   (e)  $50 \times 0.1$   (f)  $42 \times 0.003$

   (g)  $12 \div 0.1$   (h)  $140 \div 0.02$   (i)  $60 \div 0.003$

6  Without using a calculator, work out these.

   (a)  $\frac{2}{9} + \frac{3}{27}$   (b)  $\frac{3}{5} - \frac{1}{4}$

   (c)  $\frac{6}{9} \times \frac{72}{104}$   (d)  $\frac{8}{9} \div 1\frac{1}{2}$

7  Charlotte got 94 out of 126 in a maths test. What percentage is this?

8  $\frac{7}{12}$ more rain fell this year. If 156 mm fell last year, how much fell this year?

9  Reece weighed 6 lb when he was born. If his weight has increased by 65%, how much does he now weigh?

10 A house was bought for £56 000. If the price increases by 5% each year, how much will it be worth after 4 years?

11 The price of a hi-fi is reduced by 15% in the sales. It now costs £350. What was the original price?

12 A map is being enlarged in the ratio 12 : 7. If the original road length was 21 cm on the map, what is the length of the road on the enlarged map?

13 Work these out on your calculator.

   (a) $\dfrac{27.1 \times 6.4}{9.3 + 2.7}$   (b) $\dfrac{(9.3)^4}{2.7 \times 3.6}$

14 Estimate the answer to $\dfrac{(29.4)^2 + 106}{2.2 \times 5.1}$.

15 Without using a calculator, work out the cost of 135 plants at 84 pence each.

16 Without using a calculator, work out how many 13 pence chew bars Philip can buy with £3.51.

# Solving numerical problems

## Calculations

Examiner's tips and your notes

When solving problems the answers should be rounded sensibly.

**Example**

$95.26 \times 6.39 = 608.7114 = 608.71$ (2 d.p.)

*Round to 2 d.p. since the values in the question are to 2 d.p.*

**Example**

Jackie has £9.37. She divides it equally between 5 people. How much does each person receive?

$£9.37 \div 5 = £1.874$

$= £1.87$

*Round to 1.87 since it is money.*

You will lose marks if you do not write money to 2 d.p.

If the answer to a money calculation is £9.7, **always** write it to 2 d.p. as £9.70.

## Checking calculations

When checking calculations, the process can be reversed like this.

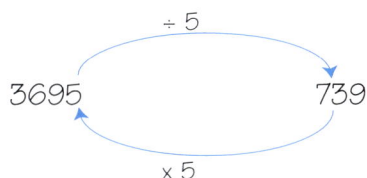

**Example**

$106 \times 3 = 318$     Check: $318 \div 3 = 106$

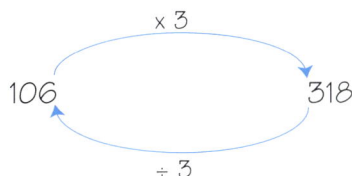

```
        ÷ 5
3695 ─────────────→ 739
        × 5
```

```
        × 3
106 ─────────────→ 318
        ÷ 3
```

## Foreign currency

The value of a single unit of currency is called the **exchange rate**.

**Example**

(a)  Find the value of £700 in Canadian dollars if there are 2.04 Canadian dollars to the pound.

(b)  What is 392 Canadian dollars in pounds sterling?

(a)  Find the **scale factor** first.

£1 = 2.04 Canadian dollars.

So £700 × 2.04 = 1428 Canadian dollars.

(b)

```
            × 2.04
£ ─────────────────→ Canadian dollars
            ÷ 2.04
```

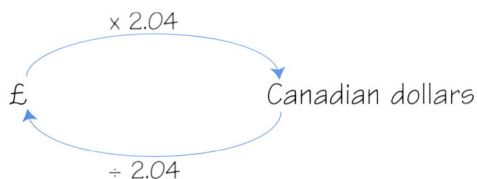

*2.04 is the scale factor.*

So $392 \div 2.04 = £192.16$ (to the nearest penny)

# Best buys

Use unit amounts to decide which is the better value for money.

### Example

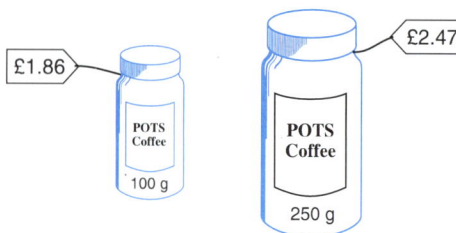

The same brand of coffee is sold in two different sized jars. Which jar represents the better value for money?

- Find the cost per gram for both jars.

  100 g costs 186p so 186 ÷ 100 = 1.86p per gram.

  250 g costs 247p so 247 ÷ 250 = 0.988p per gram.

- Since the larger jar costs less per gram it is the better value for money.

For these types of questions it is very important that each step in your working is shown, so that you can clearly justify your answer.

# Interest

## Simple interest

This is the interest that is sometimes paid on money in banks and building societies. The interest is paid each year (**per annum** or **p.a.**) and is the same amount each year.

### Example

Jonathan has £2500 in his savings account. **Simple interest** is paid at 4.4% p.a. How much does he have in his account at the end of the year?

$$100 + 4.4 = 104.4\%$$

$$\text{Total savings} = \frac{104.4}{100} \times £2500 = £2610$$

$$\text{Interest paid} = £2610 - £2500 = £110$$

This is a 'percentage of' question.

**Note:** If the money was in the account for 4 years, the interest at the end of the 4 years would be 4 × £110 = £440.

## Compound interest

This is the type of interest where the bank pays interest on the interest earned as well as on the original money.

### Example

If Jonathan has £2500 in his savings account and **compound interest** is paid at 4.4% p.a., how much will he have in his account after 4 years?

**Method 1**

Year 1: $\frac{104.4}{100}$ × £2500 = £2610

Year 2: 1.044 × 2610 = £2724.84

Year 3: 1.044 × 2724.84 = £2844.73

Year 4: 1.044 × 2844.73 = £2969.90

Total = £2969.90 (nearest penny)

**Method 2**

$\frac{104.4}{100}$ = 1.044 is the scale factor.

£2500 × 1.044 × 1.044 × 1.044 × 1.044

$\qquad$ = 2500 × (1.044)$^4$

Total = £2969.90 (nearest penny)

> Use the second method. It is much quicker.

# Tax

## National Insurance

National Insurance (NI) is usually deducted as a percentage from a wage.

> This question is just the same as finding a percentage of a quantity.

### Example
Sue earns £1402.65 a month. National Insurance at 9% is deducted. How much NI must she pay?

$\qquad$ 9% of £1402.65 = 0.09 × £1402.65 = £126.24

## Income tax

A percentage of a wage or salary is removed as income tax. **Personal allowances** must first be removed in order to obtain the **taxable income**.

### Example
Harold earns £190 per week. His first £62 is not taxable but the remainder is taxed at 24%. How much income tax does he pay each week?

| | |
|---|---|
| Taxable income | = £190 − 62 = £128 |
| 24% tax | = 0.24 × £128 = £30.72 |
| Tax per week | = £30.72 |

# Compound measures

Speed can be measured in kilometres per hour (km/h), miles per hour (m.p.h.) and metres per second (m/s). km/h, m.p.h. and m/s are all **compound measures** because they involve a combination of basic measures.

## Speed

average speed = $\dfrac{\text{total distance travelled}}{\text{total time taken}}$

$$s = \frac{d}{t}$$

> Just remember the letters. It's quicker.

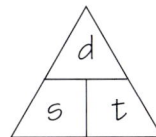

> This triangle can be used to help you remember the formulae.

Always check the units first, before starting a question. Change them if necessary.

### Example

Ruth walks 5 km in 2 hours. Find her average speed.

$$s = \frac{d}{t} = \frac{5}{2} = 2.5 \text{ km/h}$$

Since the distance is in km, time is in hours. Speed is in km/h.

### Example

A car travels 50 miles in 1 hour 20 minutes. Find the speed in miles per hour.

Change the time units first: 20 minutes = $\frac{20}{60}$ of 1 hour

$$s = \frac{d}{t} = \frac{50}{1\frac{20}{60}} = 37.5 \text{ m.p.h.}$$

Use the fraction key if possible.

From the speed formula two other formulae can be found.

$$\text{time} = \frac{\text{distance}}{\text{speed}} \qquad \text{distance} = \text{speed} \times \text{time}$$

You must learn the formulae for speed, distance and time.

$$s = \frac{d}{t} \qquad t = \frac{d}{s} \qquad d = st$$

### Example

A car travels a distance of 240 miles at an average speed of 65 m.p.h. How long does it take?

$$\text{time} = \frac{\text{distance}}{\text{speed}} \qquad \text{so } t = \frac{240}{65} = 3.692 \text{ hours}$$

3.692 hours must be changed to hours and minutes.

- Subtract the hours. So 3.692 − 3 = 0.692

- Multiply the decimal part by 60 minutes.

  0.692 × 60 = 42 minutes (nearest minute)

- Time = 3 hours 42 minutes.

## Density

$$\text{density} = \frac{\text{mass}}{\text{volume}} \qquad \text{volume} = \frac{\text{mass}}{\text{density}} \qquad \text{mass} = \text{density} \times \text{volume}$$

$$D = \frac{M}{V} \qquad V = \frac{M}{D} \qquad M = DV$$

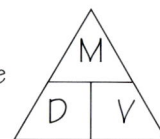

Use this triangle to help you remember the formulae.

### Example

Take care with the units.

Find the density of an object whose mass is 400 g and whose volume is 25 cm³.

$$\text{density} = \frac{M}{V} = \frac{400}{25} = 16 \text{ g/cm}^3$$

Since the mass is in grams, volume is in cm³. Density is in g/cm³.

# Solving numerical problems
## Questions

1 Nicola has £6000 in her bank account. The bank pays compound interest at the rate of 6.2% p.a. How much will she have in the bank after 3 years?

2 Katie earns £17 352 per year. £3255 is non-taxable, but the remainder is taxed at 25%.

   (a)  How much income tax does she pay?

   (b)  How much salary does she get per year after income tax has been deducted?

3 Amy walks 6 miles in 2 hours 40 minutes. Find her average speed.

4 Find the time taken for a car to travel 600 miles at an average speed of 70 m.p.h.

5 Find the density of an object whose mass is 20 grams and whose volume is 9 cm$^3$.

6 A car costs £6000 cash or can be bought by hire purchase with a 30% deposit followed by twelve monthly instalments of £365. Find:

   (a)  the deposit;

   (b)  the total amount paid for the car on hire purchase.

7 
| Super Sid's football boots $\frac{1}{3}$ off | Jungle Joe's football boots 28% off |
|---|---|

If a pair of football boots costs £49.99, which shop sells them cheaper in the sale and what is the price?

8 (a)  Karen is going to Italy. If £1 = 2355 lire. Find how many lire she will have if she changes £300 into lire for her holiday.

   (b)  After the holiday, Karen brings home 141 370 lire. What is this in Sterling?

# Functional relationships

## Formulas, expressions and substituting

**Examiner's tips and your notes**

It is important that you have a calculator that you are used to for the examination.

$p + 3$ is an **expression**.

$y = p + 3$ is a **formula**. The value of y depends on the value of p.

Replacing a letter with a number is called **substitution**. When substituting:

* Write out the expression first and then replace the letters with the values given.

* Work out the value on your calculator. Use bracket keys where possible and pay attention to the *order of operations*.

* Avoid silly answers by using **estimation** as a rough check.

### Examples

Using $w = 5.6$, $x = -7.1$ and $y = 10.8$, find the value of these expressions giving your answers to 3 s.f.

(a) $\dfrac{w + x}{y}$    (b) $w - \dfrac{x}{y}$    (c) $\sqrt{w^2 + x^2}$    (d) $wx^2$

Remember to show the substitution.

(a) $\dfrac{w + x}{y} = \dfrac{5.6 + (-7.1)}{10.8} = -0.139$

Try these out on your calculator.

When substituting into an expression or formula you must show each step in your working.

(b) $w - \dfrac{x}{y} = 5.6 - \dfrac{(-7.1)}{10.8} = 6.26$

(c) $\sqrt{w^2 + x^2} = \sqrt{5.6^2 + (-7.1)^2} = 9.04$

(d) $wx^2 = 5.6 \times (-7.1)^2 = 282$

You may need to treat $x^2$ as $(-7.1)^2$, depending on your calculator.

## Number patterns and sequences

A **sequence** is a list of numbers. There is usually a relationship between the numbers. Each value in the list is called a **term**.

### Example

The odd numbers form a sequence 1, 3, 5, 7, 9, 11,. . . in which the terms have a **common difference** of 2.

```
1       3       5       7       9      11. . .
    2       2       2       2       2
```

The common difference is 2.

## Important number sequences

| Square numbers | 1, 4, 9, 16, 25, . . . |
|---|---|
| Cube numbers | 1, 8, 27, 64, 125, . . . |
| Triangular numbers | 1, 3, 6, 10, 15, . . . |
| The Fibonacci sequence | 1, 1, 2, 3, 5, 8, 13, . . . |

## Finding the nth term of a linear sequence

The nth term is often denoted by $U_n$. For example, the 12th term is $U_{12}$.

For a linear sequence, the nth term takes the form

$$U_n = an + b$$

**Example**

For the sequence of odd numbers, find an expression for the nth term.

$$1, \quad 3, \quad 5, \quad 7, \quad 9, . . .$$

- Find the common difference; this is $a$. So $a = 2$ here.

  So $U_n = 2n + b$

- Now substitute the values of $U_1$ and $n$. $n = 1$ and $U_1 = 1$. This gives

  $1 = 2 + b$

  So $b = -1$

- nth term: $U_n = 2n - 1$

- Check: For the 10th term $U_{10} = 2 \times 10 - 1 = 19$

**Example**

Find the nth term of this sequence: 4, 7, 10, 13.

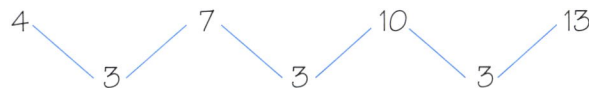

Common difference = 3, so

$U_n = 3n + b$

Substituting for $U_1$ (= 4)

$4 = (3 \times 1) + b$

$b = 1$

nth term: $U_n = 3n + 1$

Check your rule for the nth term works, by substituting another value of n into your expression.

## The $n$th term of a quadratic sequence

For a quadratic sequence the first differences are not constant, but the second differences are.

The $n$th term takes the form $U_n = an^2 + bn + c$ where $b$, $c$ may be zero.

### Example

For the sequence of triangle numbers find an expression for the $n$th term.

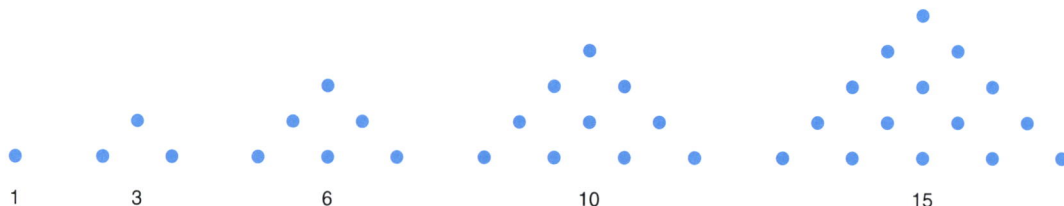

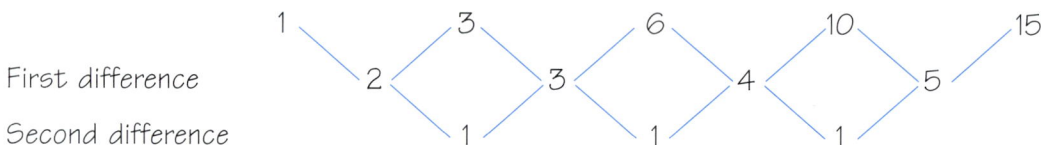

1          3          6          10          15

First difference

Second difference

1 $\diagdown$ 2 $\diagup$ 3 $\diagdown$ 3 $\diagup$ 6 $\diagdown$ 4 $\diagup$ 10 $\diagdown$ 5 $\diagup$ 15

1        1        1

- Since the second differences are the same, the rule for the $n$th term is quadratic.
- The $n$th term is $\dfrac{n^2 + n}{2}$ or $\dfrac{n(n+1)}{2}$.

> This is a useful result to remember.

# Graphs of the form $y = mx + c$

These are straight line (linear) graphs.

The general equation of a straight line graph is $y = mx + c$.

$m$ is the **gradient** (steepness) of the line.

- As $m$ increases the line gets steeper.
- If $m$ is **positive** the line slopes **forwards**.
- If $m$ is **negative** the line slopes **backwards**.

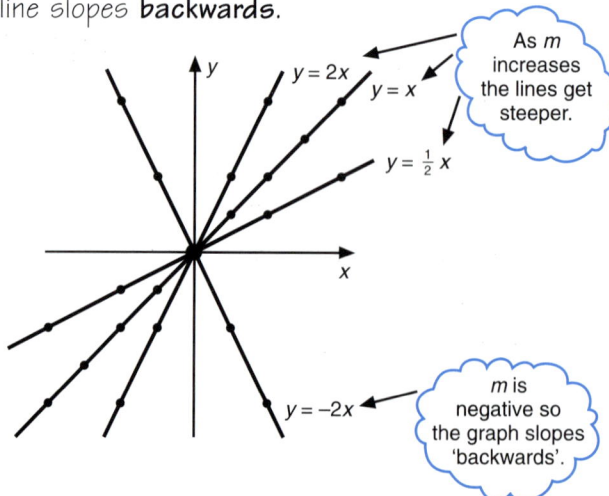

> You need to be able to sketch a straight line graph from its equation.

As $m$ increases the lines get steeper.

$m$ is negative so the graph slopes 'backwards'.

$c$ is the **intercept** on the y axis, that is, where the graph cuts the y axis.

**Parallel** lines have the **same gradient**.

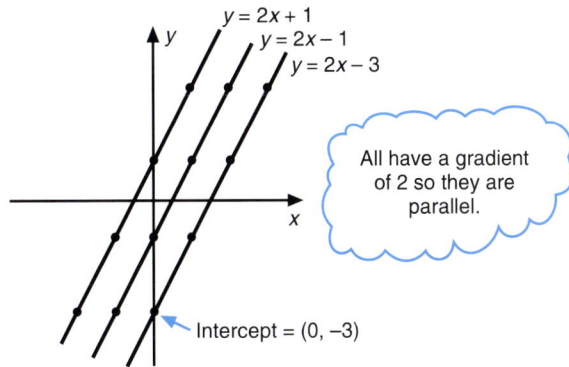

$y = 2x + 1$
$y = 2x - 1$
$y = 2x - 3$

All have a gradient of 2 so they are parallel.

Intercept = (0, −3)

## Finding the gradient of a line

Make the triangle as big as you can.

- To find the gradient, choose two points.

- Draw a triangle as shown.

- Find the change in y (height) and the change in x (base).

- gradient = $\dfrac{\text{change in y}}{\text{change in x}}$ or $\dfrac{\text{height}}{\text{base}} = \dfrac{4}{3} = 1\frac{1}{3}$

- Decide if the gradient is positive or negative.

(3, 5)

Change in y

(0, 1)

Change in x

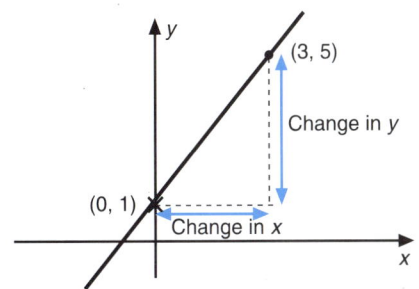

Do not count the squares as the scales may be different.

## Graphs of y = a, x = b

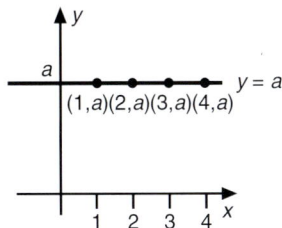

$a$

$y = a$

$(1,a)(2,a)(3,a)(4,a)$

1  2  3  4

$y = a$ is a horizontal line with every y coordinate equal to a.

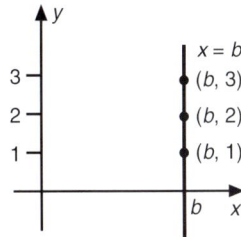

$x = b$

(b, 3)

(b, 2)

(b, 1)

$b$

$x = b$ is a vertical line with every x coordinate equal to b.

# Distance–time graphs

These are often called **travel graphs**.

The **speed** of an object can be found by finding the gradient of the line.

$$\text{speed} = \dfrac{\text{distance travelled}}{\text{time taken}}$$

Make sure you understand the scales before you start a question.

## Example

The graph shows Mr Rogers' car journey. Work out the speed of each stage.

(a)  The car is travelling at 30 m.p.h. for 1 hour (30 ÷ 1).

(b)  The car is stationary for 30 minutes.

(c)  The graph is steeper so the car is travelling faster, at a speed of 60 m.p.h. for 30 minutes (30 ÷ 0.5).

(d)  The car is stationary for 1 hour.

(e)  The return journey is at a speed of 40 m.p.h. (60 ÷ 1.5).

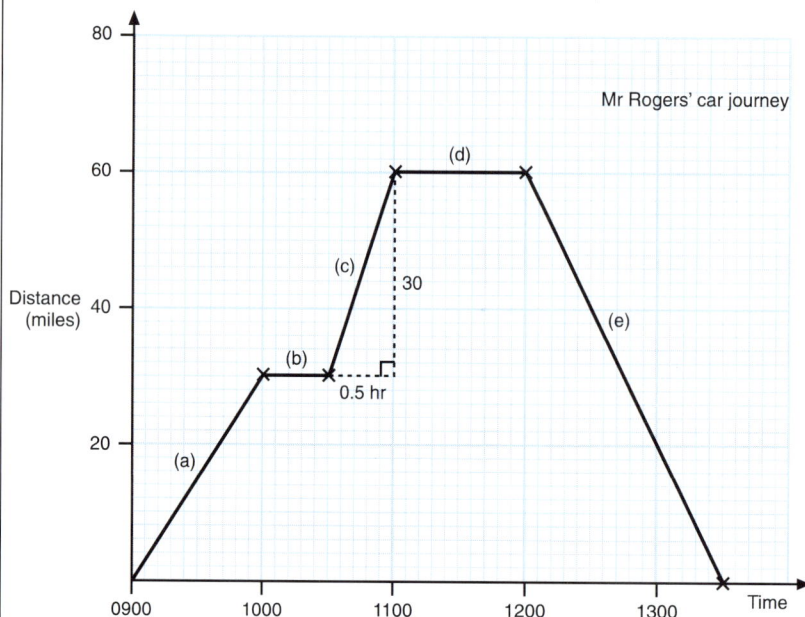

Note that each small square on the horizontal axis represents 6 minutes on this graph.

# Graphs of the form $y = ax^2 + bx + c$

These are called **quadratic graphs** where $a \neq 0$.

These graphs are curved.

They are often known as **parabolas**.

If $a > 0$ then the graph is shaped as shown.

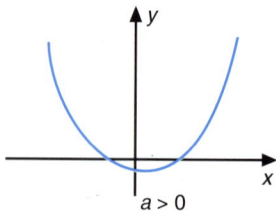

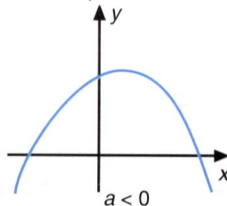

$a > 0$

If $a < 0$ then the graph is shaped as shown.

$a < 0$

## Example

Draw the graph of $y = x^2 - x - 6$ using values of $x$ from −2 to 3.

Use the graph to find the value of $x$ when $y = -3$.

- Make a table of values.

| x | −2 | −1 | 0 | 1 | 2 | 3 | 0.5 |
|---|---|---|---|---|---|---|---|
| y | 0 | −4 | −6 | −6 | −4 | 0 | −6.25 |

$x = 0.5$ is worked out to find the minimum value.

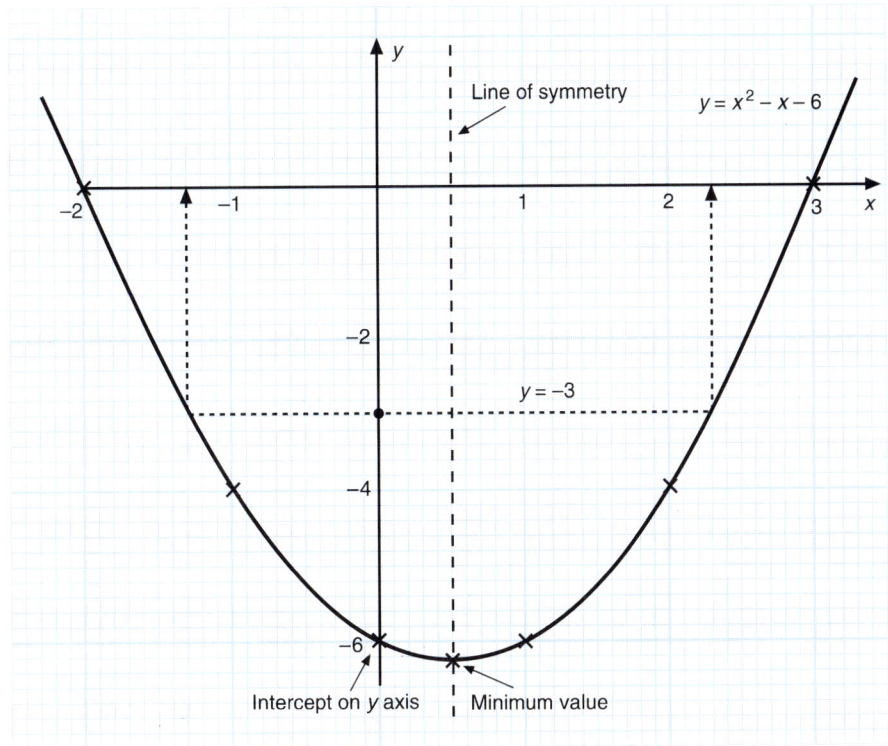

Line of symmetry

$y = x^2 - x - 6$

$y = -3$

Intercept on y axis    Minimum value

Draw the curve with a sharp pencil, go through all the points and check for any points that look wrong.

- Plot the points and join with a smooth curve.

- The minimum value is when x = 0.5, y = −6.25.

- The line of symmetry is at x = 0.5.

- The curve cuts the y axis at (0, −6), i.e. (0, c).

- When y = −3, read across from y = −3 to the graph then read up to the x axis. x = 2.3 and x = −1.3. These are the approximate **solutions** of the equation $x^2 - x - 6 = -3$.

# Graphs involving $x^3$ and $\frac{1}{x}$

An equation of the form $y = ax^3 + bx^2 + cx + d$ is called a **cubic** where $a \neq 0$.

For $a > 0$ the graph of a cubic takes one of these forms.

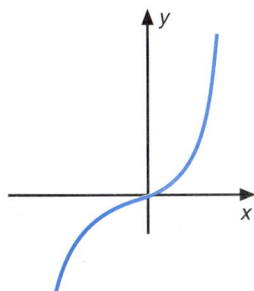

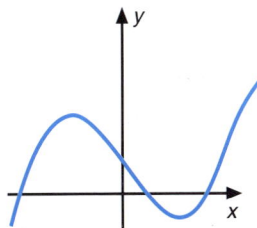

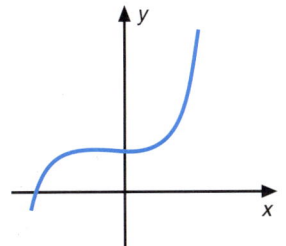

For $a < 0$ the overall trend is reversed.

The basic shapes of all of these graphs need to be learnt.

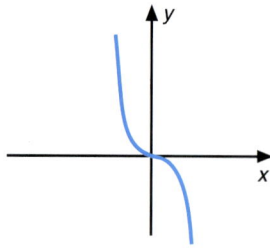

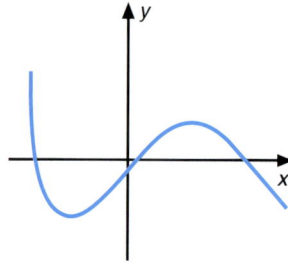

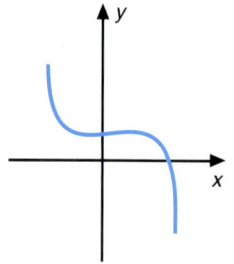

An equation of the form $y = \dfrac{a}{x}$ takes two basic forms depending on the value of $a$.

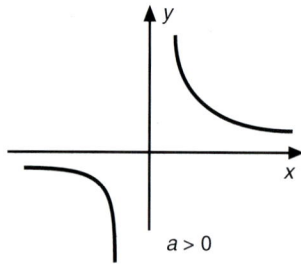

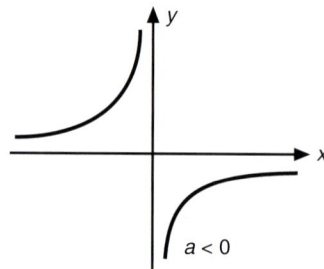

$a > 0$

$a < 0$

## Example

Draw the graph of $P = \dfrac{18}{V}$ for values of $V$ from 1 to 6. Find the value of $V$ if $P = 8$.

- Draw the table of values first.

| $V$ | 1 | 2 | 3 | 4 | 5 | 6 |
|-----|----|---|---|-----|-----|---|
| $P$ | 18 | 9 | 6 | 4.5 | 3.6 | 3 |

- Find the values of $P$ by dividing 18 by $V$.

- Draw a smooth curve through the points.

- To find $V$ when $P = 8$ read across at $P = 8$ then draw a line down. $V \approx 2.24$.

Show clearly on your graph how you have taken the reading.

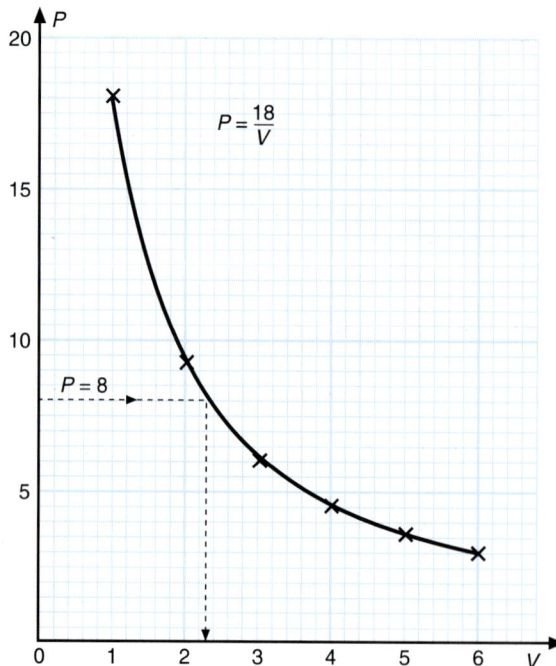

# Functional relationships
## Questions

1 If $a = 3.6$, $b = -2.4$ and $c = 6.1$, find the value of these expressions giving your answers to 3 significant figures.

(a) $3a - 4b$  (b) $2b^2 + 3c$

(c) $ab^2$  (d) $c + \dfrac{a}{b}$

2 Find the $n$th term of these sequences:  (a) 5, 9, 13, 17  (b) 3, 6, 11, 18

3 Write down the gradient and intercept of each of these straight line graphs:

(a) $y = 4x - 1$  (b) $y = 3 - 2x$  (c) $2y = 4x + 8$

4 The travel graph shows the car journeys of two people. From the travel graph find:

(a) the speed at which Miss Young is travelling;

(b) the length of time Mr Price has a break;

(c) the speed of Mr Price from London to Birmingham;

(d) the time at which Miss Young and Mr Price pass each other.

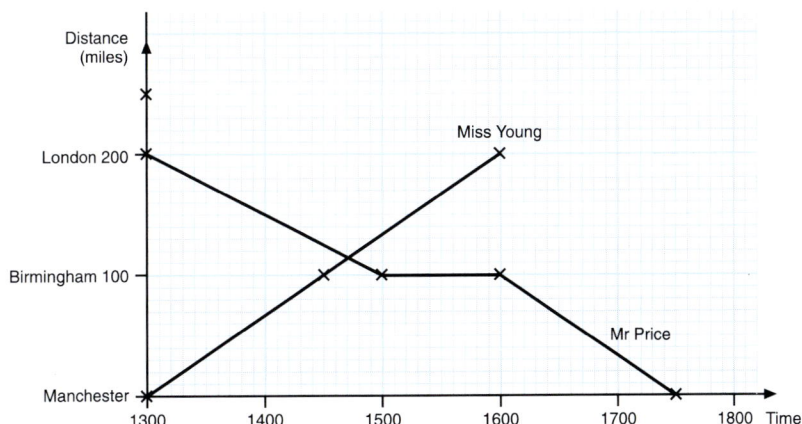

5 (a) Complete the table of values for the graph $y = x^3 + 3$.

| x | −3 | −2 | −1 | 0 | 1 | 2 | 3 |
|---|----|----|----|---|---|---|---|
| y |    |    |    |   |   |   |   |

(b) Draw the graph of $y = x^3 + 3$. Use scales of 1 unit per 2 cm on the x axis and 10 units per 2 cm on the y axis.

(c) From the graph find the value of x when $y = 15$.

6 Match each of the four graphs below with one of the following equations:

(a) $y = 2x - 5$  (b) $y = x^2 + 3$  (c) $y = 3 - x^2$  (d) $y = 5 - x$  (e) $y = x^3$  (f) $y = \dfrac{2}{x}$

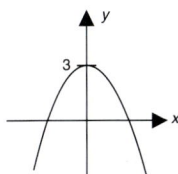

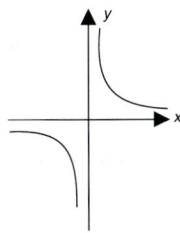

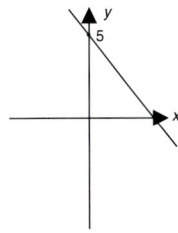

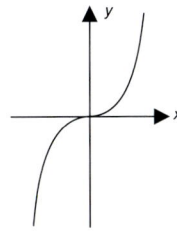

Graph A          Graph B          Graph C          Graph D

# Equations and formulae

## Algebraic conventions

Examiner's tips and your notes

$3 \times a$ is written without the multiplication sign as $3a$.

$a + a + a = 3a$

$a \times a \times a = a^3$, not $3a$

$a \times a \times 2 = 2a^2$, not $(2a)^2$

$a \times b \times 2 = 2ab$

*Put the number first, then the letters in alphabetical order.*

## Using formulae

Formulae describe expressions. A formula must have an = sign in it.

### Example
Andrew hires a van. There is a standing charge of £8 and then it costs £3 per hour. How much does it cost for:

(a)  6 hours' hire;          (b)  y hours' hire?

(c)  Write a formula for the total hire cost C.

(a)  $8 + (3 \times 6) = £26$

(b)  $8 + (3 \times y) = 8 + 3y$

(c)  $C = 8 + 3y$

*This is a formula which works out the cost of hiring the van for any number of hours.*

*Make sure you include an equals sign in your formula.*

## Collecting like terms

Expressions can be simplified by collecting **like terms**.

Only collect the terms if their letters and powers are **identical**.

### Examples

$4a + 2a = 6a$

$3a^2 + 6a^2 - 4a^2 = 5a^2$

$4a + 6b - 3a + 2b = a + 8b$

$9a + 4b$ cannot be simplified since there are no like terms.

$3xy + 2yx = 5xy$

*Add the as, then the bs. Remember a means 1a.*

*Remember xy means the same as yx.*

# Indices

The rules that apply with numbers also apply with letters.

## The laws of indices

These rules are not given on the formulae sheet in the examination and so they must be learnt.

$a^n \times a^m = a^{n+m}$    $a^n \div a^m = a^{n-m}$    $(a^n)^m = a^{n \times m}$    $a^0 = 1$    $a^1 = a$

### Examples

$4x^2 \times 3x^5 = 12x^7$    $15x^9 \div 3x^2 = 5x^7$    $(2x^4)^3 = 8x^{12}$

Note that the numbers are multiplied,... ...but the powers of the same letter are added.

# Multiplying out brackets

This helps to simplify algebraic expressions.

Multiply everything inside the bracket by everything outside the bracket.

$a(b + c - d) = ab + ac - ad$

If you are asked to expand brackets it just means multiply out.

### Examples

$3(2x + 5) = 6x + 15$        $(3 \times 2x = 6x, 3 \times 5 = 15)$

$a(3a - 4) = 3a^2 - 4a$        $b(2a + 3b - c) = 2ab + 3b^2 - bc$

If the term outside the bracket is **negative**, all of the signs of the terms inside the bracket are **changed** when multiplying out.

Remember the rules for multiplying by negative numbers.

### Examples

$-4(2x + 3) = -8x - 12$    $-2(4 - 3x) = -8 + 6x$

To simplify expressions expand the brackets first then collect like terms.

### Example

Expand and simplify $2(x - 3) + x(x + 4)$.

$2(x - 3) + x(x + 4)$        Multiply out the brackets.

$= 2x - 6 + x^2 + 4x$        Collect like terms.

$= x^2 + 6x - 6$

## Multiplication of two brackets

Each term in the first bracket is multiplied with each term in the second bracket.

If you are asked to simplify you must collect like terms.

**Examples**

Expand and simplify the following.

(a)  $(x + 2)(x + 3)$

$= x(x + 3) + 2(x + 3)$

$= x^2 + 3x + 2x + 6$

$= x^2 + 5x + 6$

Each term in the first bracket is multiplied with the second, simplify by collecting like terms.

(b)  $(2x + 4)(3x - 2)$

$= 2x(3x - 2) + 4(3x - 2)$

$= 6x^2 - 4x + 12x - 8$

$= 6x^2 + 8x - 8$

(c)  $(x + y)^2$

$= x(x + y) + y(x + y)$

$= x^2 + xy + xy + y^2$

$= x^2 + 2xy + y^2$

A common error is to think that $(a + b)^2$ means $a^2 + b^2$.

# Factorisation

This is the reverse of expanding brackets. An expression is put into brackets by taking out **common factors**.

## One bracket

expand

$y(x + 4)$         $xy + 4y$

factorise

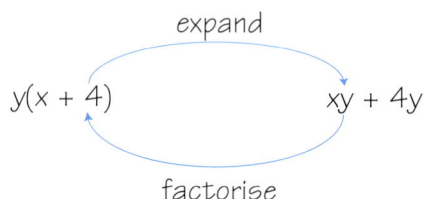

To factorise $xy + 4y$:

- recognise that $y$ is a factor of each term;

- take out the common factor;

- the expression is completed inside the bracket, so that the result is equivalent to $xy + 4y$, when multiplied out.

After factorising check that you obtain the original expression by multiplying out the brackets.

**Examples**

Factorise the following.

(a)  $5x^2 + x = x(5x + 1)$

(b)  $4x^2 + 8x = 4x(x + 2)$

Highest factor of 4 and 8 is taken out.

(c)  $5x^3 + 15x^4 = 5x^3(1 + 3x)$

## Two brackets

Two brackets are obtained when a quadratic expression of the type $x^2 + bx + c$ is factorised.

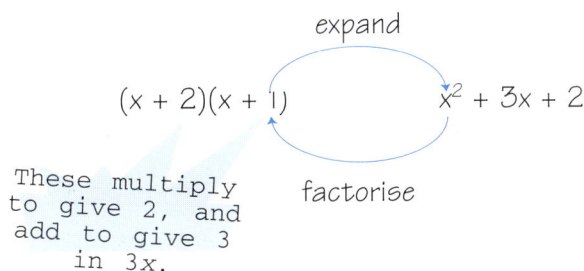

expand

$$(x + 2)(x + 1) \qquad x^2 + 3x + 2$$

These multiply to give 2, and add to give 3 in $3x$.

factorise

### Examples

Factorise the following.

(a) $x^2 + 5x - 6 = (x - 1)(x + 6)$

(b) $x^2 - 6x + 8 = (x - 2)(x - 4)$

(c) $x^2 - 16 = (x - 4)(x + 4)$

# Rearranging formulae

The **subject** of a formula is the letter that appears on its own on one side of the formula.

### Examples

Make $p$ the subject of these formulae:  (a) $r = (p + 6)^2$  (b) $y = \dfrac{p + r}{6}$

Remember to show each step in your working.

(a) $r = (p + 6)^2$     Deal with the power first. Take the square root of both sides.

$\sqrt{r} = p + 6$     Remove any terms added or subtracted. So subtract 6 from both sides.

$\sqrt{r} - 6 = p$

(b) $y = \dfrac{p + r}{6}$     Deal with the value dividing with $p$; multiply both sides by 6.

$6y = p + r$     Remove $r$ by subtracting $r$ from both sides.

$6y - r = p$ or $p = 6y - r$     The subject of the formula is usually written first.

# Linear equations

An equation involves an unknown value which has to be worked out.

The **balance** method is usually used; whatever is done to one side of an equation must be done to the other.

## Examples

Solve the following.

(a)  $\frac{x}{6} + 1 = 3$

$\frac{x}{6} = 3 - 1$      Subtract 1 from both sides.

$\frac{x}{6} = 2$      Multiply both sides by 6.

$x = 12$

(b)  $8x - 6 = 4x + 1$

$4x - 6 = 1$      Subtract 4x from both sides.

$4x = 7$      Add 6 to both sides.

$x = \frac{7}{4} = 1\frac{3}{4}$      Divide both sides by 4.

(c)  $3(x - 2) = 2(x + 6)$      Multiply brackets out first.

$3x - 6 = 2x + 12$

$x - 6 = 12$

$x = 18$

(d)  $5(x - 2) + 6 = 3(x - 4) + 10$

$5x - 10 + 6 = 3x - 12 + 10$

$5x - 4 = 3x - 2$

$2x - 4 = -2$

$2x = 2$

$x = 1$

# Simultaneous equations

Two equations with two unknowns are called **simultaneous equations**.

They can be solved in several ways. Solving equations simultaneously involves finding values for the letters that will make both equations work.

## Graphical method

The points at which any two graphs **intersect** represent the simultaneous solutions of these equations.

### Example

Solve the simultaneous equations $y = 2x - 1$, $x + y = 5$

- Draw the two graphs.

  $y = 2x - 1$    If $x = 0$, $y = -1$

             If $y = 0$, $x = \frac{1}{2}$

  $x + y = 5$    If $x = 0$, $y = 5$

             If $y = 0$, $x = 5$

- At the point of intersection $x = 2$ and $y = 3$.

  These values represent the simultaneous solutions of $y = 2x - 1$ and $x + y = 5$

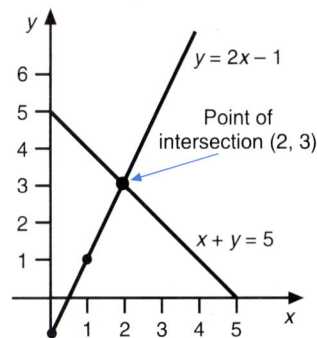

## Elimination method

If the coefficient of one of the letters is the same in both equations, then that letter may be eliminated by subtracting the equations.

The **coefficient** is the number a letter is multiplied by; e.g. the coefficient of $-2x$ is $-2$.

### Example

Solve simultaneously    $2x + 3y = 6$ and $x + y = 1$

$2x + 3y = 6$    ①    Label the equations ① and ②.

$x + y = 1$    ②    As no coefficients match, multiply equation ② by 2.

$2x + 2y = 2$    ③    The coefficients of $x$ are now the same in equations ① and ③.

$0x + y = 4$        Subtract equation ③ from equation ①.

So $y = 4$

$x + 4 = 1$ so $x = -3$    Substitute the value of $y = 4$ into equation ① or equation ②.

*Always check that the values work.*

Check in equation 1: $(2 \times -3) + (3 \times 4) = 6$

Substitute $x = -3$ and $y = 4$ into the other equation.

The solution is $x = -3$, $y = 4$

To eliminate terms with **opposite** signs, **add**.

To eliminate terms with the **same** signs, **subtract**.

# Solving quadratic equations

Make sure the quadratic equation is equal to zero. Then factorise the quadratic equation.

### Examples

Solve the following.

(a)   $x^2 - 5x = 0$        $x$ is a common factor.

     $x(x - 5) = 0$

     Either $x = 0$

     or $x - 5 = 0$, i.e. $x = 5$

In order for this to be zero, either $x = 0$ or $(x - 5) = 0$

(b)  $x^2 - 3x = 10$
   $x^2 - 3x - 10 = 0$          Make it equal to zero and factorise.
   $(x + 2)(x - 5) = 0$
   Either $(x + 2) = 0$ i.e. $x = -2$
   or $(x - 5) = 0$ i.e. $x = 5$

# Solving cubic equations by trial and improvement

Trial and improvement gives an approximate solution to equations. It involves a systematic search, whereby selected values are substituted into one side of the equation in order to reach some target figure on the other.

### Example

The equation $x^3 - 5x = 10$ has a solution between 2 and 3. Find this solution to 2 decimal places.

Draw a table to help.

Substitute different values of x into $x^3 - 5x$.

Make sure you write down the solution of $x$, not the answer to $x^3 - 5x$.

| $x$ | $x^3 - 5x$ | Comment |
|---|---|---|
| 2.5 | 3.125 | too small |
| 2.8 | 7.952 | too small |
| 2.9 | 9.889 | too small |
| 2.95 | 10.922375 | too big |
| 2.94 | 10.712184 | too big |
| 2.91 | 10.092171 | too big |

At this stage the solution is trapped between 2.90 and 2.91. Checking the middle value $x = 2.905$ gives $x^3 - 5x = 9.99036 \ldots$ which is too small.

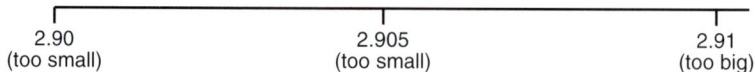

```
    2.90              2.905              2.91
 (too small)       (too small)        (too big)
```

The diagram makes it clear that the solution is 2.91 correct to 2 decimal places.

# Inequalities

These are expressions where one side is **not equal** to the other.

Inequalities are solved in a similar way to equations.

$<$ 'is less than',
$>$ 'is greater than'
$\leq$ 'is less than or equal to'
$\geq$ 'is greater than or equal to'

44

Multiplying and dividing by **negative numbers** changes the **direction** of the sign. For example if $-x \geq 5$ then $x \leq -5$.

### Examples

Solve the following inequalities.

(a) $4x - 2 < 2x + 6$

| | |
|---|---|
| $2x - 2 < 6$ | Subtract $2x$ from both sides. |
| $2x < 8$ | Add 2 to both sides. |
| $x < 4$ | Divide both sides by 2. |

The solution of the inequality may be represented on a number line.

> Solve inequalities in a similar way to equations.

> Use • when the end point is included and ○ when the end point is not included.

(b) $-5 < 3x + 1 \leq 13$      Subtract 1 from each side.

$-6 < 3x \leq 12$      Divide by 3.

$-2 < x \leq 4$

The **integer values** which satisfy the above inequality are $-1, 0, 1, 2, 3, 4$.

## Graphs of inequalities

The graph of an equation such as $y = 3$ is a line, whereas the graph of the inequality $y < 3$ is a **region** which has the line $y = 3$ as its **boundary**.

To show the region for given inequalities:

- Draw the boundary lines first.

- For **strict** inequalities $>$ and $<$ the boundary line is not included and is shown as a dotted line.

- It is often easier with several inequalities to shade out the unwanted regions, so that the solution is shown **unshaded**.

### Example

The diagram shows unshaded the region $x > 1$, $x + y \leq 4$, $y \geq 0$

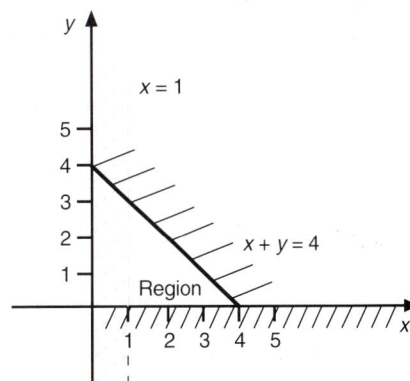

# Questions

1  Simplify:

   (a)  $4x^2 \times 5x^3$                (b)  $6x^{13} \div 2x^9$

   (c)  $(4x^3)^2$                        (d)  $x^0$

2  Expand and simplify:

   (a)  $2(x - 6) + 3x(x - 2)$            (b)  $(x + 6)(x - 2)$

   (c)  $(x - 6)^2$                       (d)  $(2x + y)(3x - 2)$

3  Factorise the following expressions.

   (a)  $pq + qr$            (b)  $5x^2 + 10x^3y$

   (c)  $x^2 - 5x + 4$       (d)  $x^2 - 64$

4  Make $a$ the subject of each formula.

   (a)  $r = 5a$             (b)  $r = \sqrt{4a + b}$       (c)  $r = 4q - 2a$

5  Solve the following equations.

   (a)  $4x - 3 = 9$                      (b)  $6x + 3 = 2x + 9$

   (c)  $5(x - 4) = 3(x - 6)$             (d)  $\dfrac{500}{x} = 10$

6  Solve the simultaneous equations:   $3a + b = 5$

$2a + 3b = 1$

7  Solve these quadratic equations.

   (a)  $x^2 - 7x = 0$       (b)  $x^2 = 9x - 20$

8  Solve these inequalities.

   (a)  $5x - 1 \le 2x + 9$       (b)  $-4 < 2x - 6 \le 10$

## Properties of shapes

## Symmetry

### Reflective symmetry

Both sides of a symmetrical shape are the same when the mirror line is drawn across it. The mirror line is known as the **line** or **axis of symmetry**.

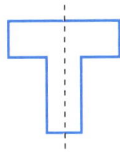

1 line

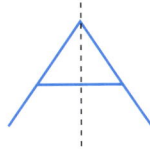

1 line

3 lines

No lines

### Rotational symmetry

A 2D (two-dimensional) shape has rotational symmetry, if, when it is turned, it looks exactly the same. The **order of rotational symmetry** is the number of times the shape turns and looks the same.

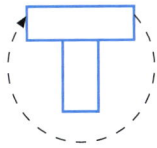

Order 1

Order 1

Order 3

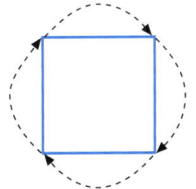

Order 4

For the letter M the shape has 1 position. It is said to have **rotational symmetry of order 1**, or **no** rotational symmetry.

### Plane symmetry

This is symmetry in 3D (three-dimensional) solids only.

A 3D shape has a **plane of symmetry** if the plane divides the shape into two halves, and one half is an exact mirror image of the other.

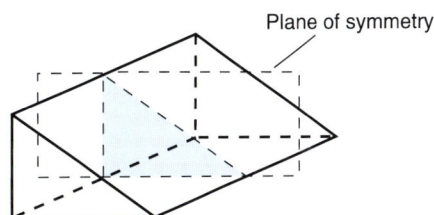

Plane of symmetry

# 2D shapes

## Triangles

There are several types of triangle.

**Equilateral**

**Isosceles**

**Right-angled**

**Scalene**

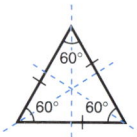

3 sides equal
3 angles equal

2 sides equal
base angles equal

has a 90° angle

no sides or angles
the same

## Quadrilaterals

*You must learn the names of these shapes and their symmetrical properties.*

These are four-sided shapes.

**Square**

**Rectangle**

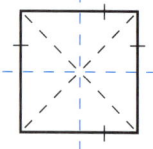

4 lines of symmetry
rotational symmetry of order 4

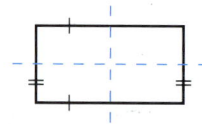

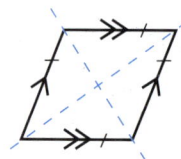

2 lines of symmetry
rotational symmetry of order 2

**Parallelogram**

**Rhombus**

no lines of symmetry
rotational symmetry of order 2

2 lines of symmetry
rotational symmetry of order 2

**Kite**

**Trapezium**

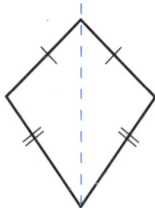

1 line of symmetry
no rotational symmetry

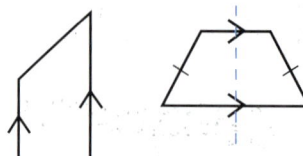

isosceles trapezium:
1 line of symmetry
no rotational symmetry

## Polygons

These are 2D shapes with **straight** sides.

**Regular polygons** are shapes with all sides and angles equal.

| Number of sides | Name of polygon |
|---|---|
| 3 | Triangle |
| 4 | Quadrilateral |
| 5 | Pentagon |
| 6 | Hexagon |
| 7 | Heptagon |
| 8 | Octagon |
| 9 | Nonagon |
| 10 | Decagon |

## Circle

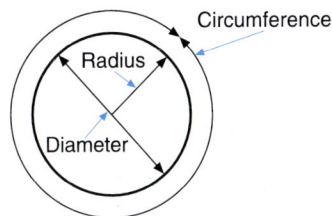

diameter = 2 × radius

The **circumference** is the distance around the outside edge.

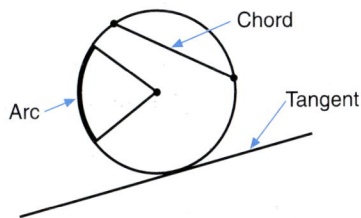

A **chord** is a line that joins two points on the circumference. The line does not go through the centre.

A **tangent** touches the circle at one point only.

An **arc** is part of the circumference.

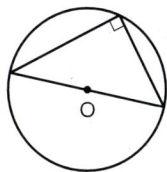

The angle in a semicircle is always a right angle.

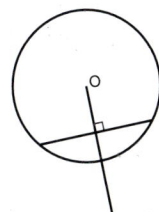

The **perpendicular bisector** of a chord passes through the centre of a circle.

## Congruent shapes

These are 2D shapes which are exactly the same size and shape.

# 3D shapes

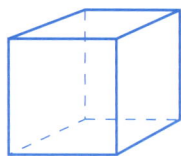
Cube

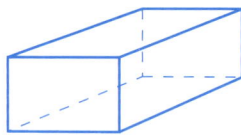
Cuboid

Sphere

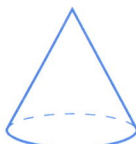
Cylinder

Cone

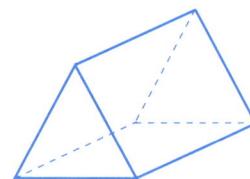
Triangular prism

You must learn the mathematical names of all of these 3D shapes.

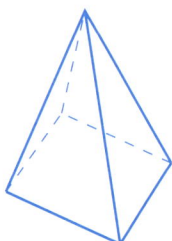
Square-based pyramid

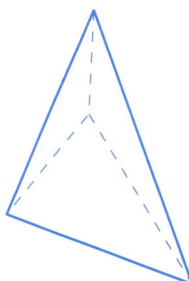
Triangular-based pyramid (tetrahedron)

# Drawing shapes

## Nets of solids

The net of a 3D shape is the 2D shape which is folded to make the 3D shape.

**Examples**

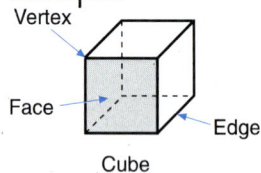
Vertex
Face
Edge
Cube

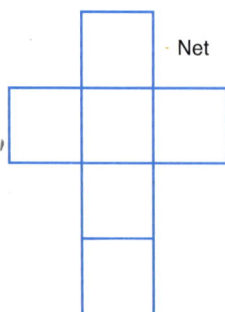
Net

Square-based pyramid

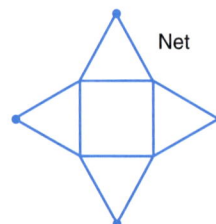
Net

If you were making the shape you would need tabs for sticking.

## Plans and elevations

A **plan** is what is seen if a 3D shape is looked down on from above.

An **elevation** is seen if the 3D shape is looked at from the side, or front.

When drawing plans and elevations of 3D shapes, measure and draw them carefully.

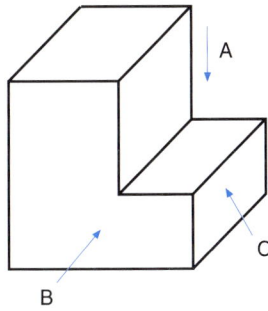

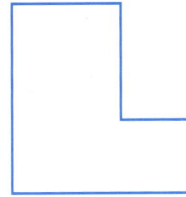

Plan          Front elevation          Side elevation

## Constructing a triangle

### Example

Use compasses to construct this triangle.

- Draw the longest side.
- With the compass point at A, draw an arc of radius 4 cm.
- With the compass point at B, draw an arc of radius 5 cm.
- Join A and B to the point where the two arcs meet at C.

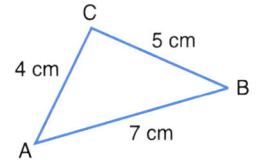

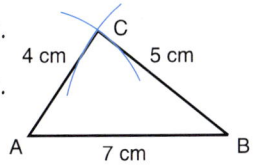

# Angles

An **acute** angle is between 0° and 90°.

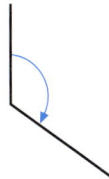

An **obtuse** angle is between 90° and 180°.

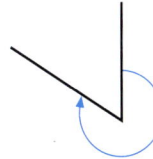

A **reflex** angle is between 180° and 360°.

A **right angle** is 90°.

# Angle facts

Try to remember these angle facts.

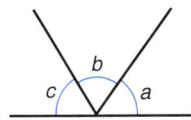

Angles on a **straight line** add up to **180°**.
$a + b + c = 180°$

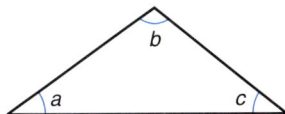

Angles at a **point** add up to **360°**.
$a + b + c + d = 360°$

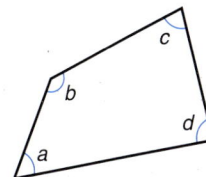

Angles in a **triangle** add up to **180°**.
$a + b + c = 180°$

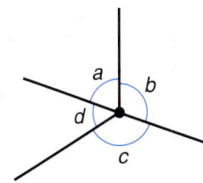

Angles in a **quadrilateral** add up to **360°**.
$a + b + c + d = 360°$

51

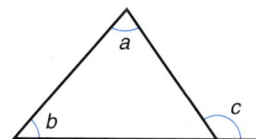

**Vertically opposite** angles are **equal**.
$a = b, c = d$
$a + d = b + c = 180°$

An **exterior angle** of a triangle equals the sum of the **two** opposite **interior angles**.
$a + b = c$

## Angles in parallel lines

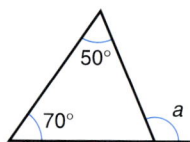

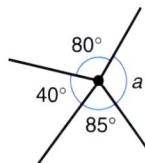

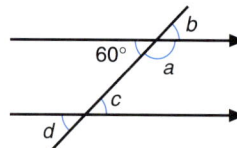

**Alternate** (z) angles are **equal**.

**Corresponding** angles are **equal**.

**Supplementary** angles add up to **180°**.
$c + d = 180°$

**Examples**

Find the angles labelled by letters.

Remember to show all of your working out.

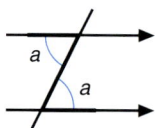

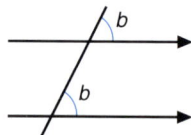

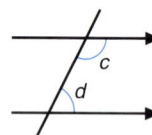

$a = 50° + 70°$

$a = 120°$

$a + 80° + 40° + 85° = 360°$

$a = 360° - 205°$

$a = 155°$

$a = 120°$ (angles on a straight line)

$b = 60°$ (vertically opposite)

$c = 60°$ (corresponding to $b$)

$d = 60°$ (vertically opposite to $c$)

## Reading angles

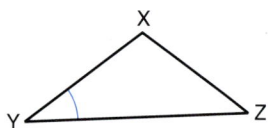

When asked to find XYZ or $\angle$XYZ or $X\hat{Y}Z$, find the **middle letter** angle, angle Y.

## Angles in polygons

There are two types of angle in a polygon: **interior** (inside) and **exterior** (outside).

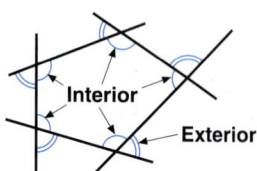

For a regular polygon with $n$ sides:

- sum of exterior angles = 360°, so exterior angle = **360°/$n$**

- interior angle + exterior angle = 180°

- sum of interior angles = **($n$ − 2) × 180°**

## Example

A regular polygon has an interior angle of 150°. How many sides does it have?

Let $n$ be the number of sides.

exterior + interior = 180°

exterior angle = 180° − 150° = 30°

But exterior angle = $\dfrac{360°}{n}$

So $n = \dfrac{360°}{\text{exterior angle}}$

$n = \dfrac{360°}{30°} = 12$

The polygon has 12 sides.

# Pythagoras' theorem

Pythagoras' theorem allows us to calculate one of the sides when the other two are known.

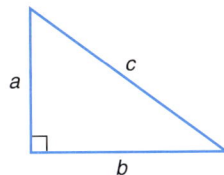

The **hypotenuse** is the longest side of a right-angled triangle. It is always opposite the right angle.

Pythagoras' theorem states: in any right-angled triangle, the square on the hypotenuse is equal to the sum of the squares on the other two sides.

Using the letters in the diagram, the theorem is written as:

$$c^2 = a^2 + b^2$$

This may be rearranged to give $a^2 = c^2 - b^2$ or $b^2 = c^2 - a^2$, which are useful when calculating one of the shorter sides.

## Example

Find the length of AB, giving your answer to 1 decimal place.

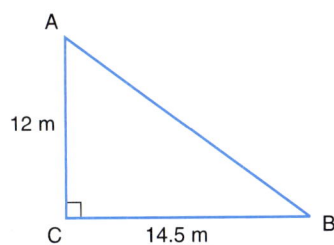

If you are not told to what degree of accuracy to round your answer, be guided by significant figures given in the question.

Using Pythagoras' theorem gives:

$AB^2 = AC^2 + BC^2$
$\quad\;\; = 12^2 + 14.5^2$
$\quad\;\; = 354.25$
$AB = \sqrt{354.25}$  Square root to find AB.
$\quad\;\; = 18.8\,\text{m (to 1 d.p.)}$  Round to 1 d.p.

## Example

Find the length of FG, giving your answer to 1 d.p.

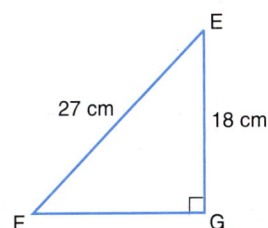

Using Pythagoras' theorem gives:

Rearrange the formula: use $a^2 = c^2 - b^2$

$EF^2 = EG^2 + FG^2$
$FG^2 = EF^2 - EG^2$
$\quad\;\; = 27^2 - 18^2$
$\quad\;\; = 405$
$FG = \sqrt{405}$
$\quad\;\; = 20.1\,\text{cm (to 1 d.p.)}$

# Trigonometry in right-angled triangles

Trigonometry in right-angled triangles can be used to calculate an unknown angle or an unknown length.

## Labelling the sides of the triangle

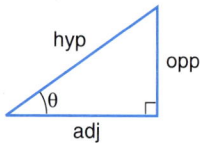

**hyp** (hypotenuse) is opposite the right angle.

**opp** (opposite side) is opposite the angle θ.

**adj** (adjacent side) is next to the angle θ.

## Trigonometric ratios

The trigonometric ratios are given on the GCSE formula sheet.

$$\sin θ = \frac{opp}{hyp} \qquad \cos θ = \frac{adj}{hyp} \qquad \tan θ = \frac{opp}{adj}$$

## Calculating the length of a side

**Example**

To help you decide on which ratio to use, circle the sides which are needed.

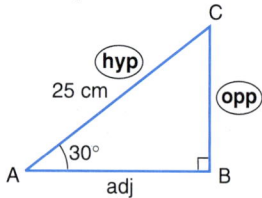

Calculate the length of BC.

- Label the sides first.

- Decide on the ratio.

$$\sin 30° = \frac{opp}{hyp}$$

- Substitute in the values.

$$\sin 30° = \frac{BC}{25}$$

$$25 × \sin 30° = BC \qquad \text{Multiply both sides by 25.}$$

$$BC = 12.5 \text{ cm}$$

**Example**

Take extra care when the length you are trying to find is on the bottom.

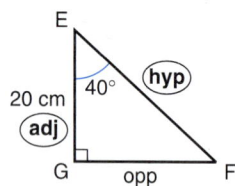

Calculate the length of EF.

$$\cos 40° = \frac{adj}{hyp} = \frac{20}{EF}$$

$$EF × \cos 40° = 20 \qquad \text{Multiply both sides by EF.}$$

$$EF = \frac{20}{\cos 40°} \qquad \text{Divide both sides by } \cos 40°.$$

$$= 26.1 \text{ cm (1 d.p.)}$$

## Calculating the size of an angle

### Example

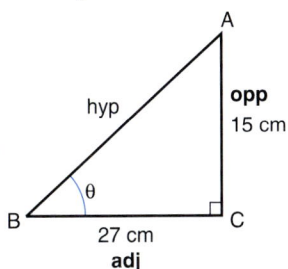

Calculate angle $A\hat{B}C$.

$\tan \theta = \dfrac{opp}{adj}$    Label the sides and decide on the ratio.

$\tan \theta = \dfrac{15}{27}$    Divide the top value by the bottom value.

$\tan \theta = 0.\dot{5}$

$\theta = 29.1°$ (1 d.p.)

## Angles of elevation and depression

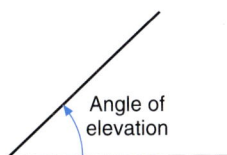

The **angle of elevation** is measured from the horizontal **upwards**.

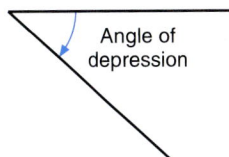

The **angle of depression** is measured from the horizontal **downwards**.

### Example

Dipak stands 30 m from the base of a tower. He measures the angle of elevation from ground level to the top of the tower as 50°. Calculate the height of the tower. Give your answer to 3 s.f.

$\tan 50° = \dfrac{opp}{adj} = \dfrac{height}{30}$

$30 \times \tan 50° = $ height of tower

height of tower $= 35.8$ m (3 s.f.)

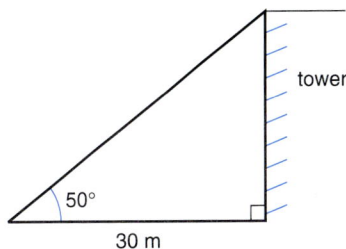

tower

50°

30 m

# Questions

1 What is the name of an eight-sided polygon?

2 Draw a quick sketch of the main 3D shapes and give them their mathematical name. (You need to know 8.)

3 Draw the net of this cuboid.

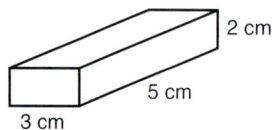

4 Find the sizes of the angles labelled by letters.

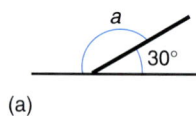

(a)

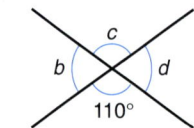

(b)

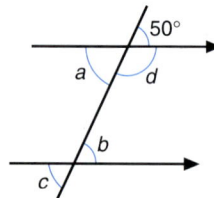

(c)

5 Find the size of an (a) exterior, (b) interior angle of a regular pentagon.

6 Calculate the lengths of the sides marked with a letter. Give your answers to 1 d.p.

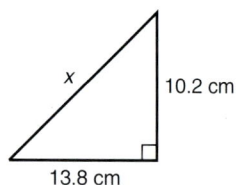

(a)

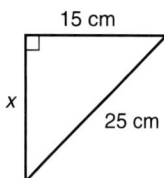

(b)

7

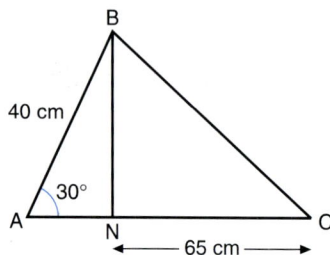

(a) Calculate the length of BN.

(b) Calculate the length of BC.

(c) Calculate the size of ∠BCN.

# Properties of position, movement and transformation

## Tessellations

Examiner's tips and your notes

A **tessellation** is a pattern of 2D shapes which fit together without leaving any gaps.

For shapes to tessellate, the angles at each point must add up to 360°.

### Example

Regular pentagons will not tessellate.
Each interior angle is 108°, and

$3 \times 108° = 324°$

A gap of $360° - 324° = 36°$ is left.

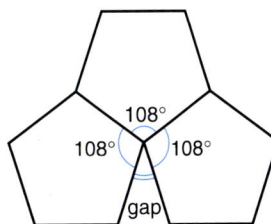

## Bearings

Bearings give a direction in degrees.

Bearings are always measured from the **north** in a **clockwise** direction. They must have 3 figures.

### Examples

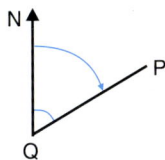

Bearing of P **from** Q
= 060°

Measure from the north line at Q.

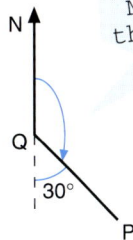

Bearing of P from Q
= 180° − 30° = 150°

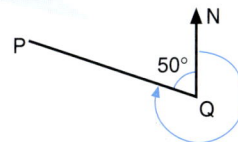

Bearing of P from Q
360° − 50° = 310°

The word 'from' is important. It tells you where to put the north line and measure from.

When finding the **back bearing** (the bearing of Q **from** P above):

• draw in a north line at P;

• the two north lines are parallel lines, so the angle properties of parallel lines are used.

### Examples

Measure from the north line at P.

Look for alternate or corresponding angles when finding back bearings.

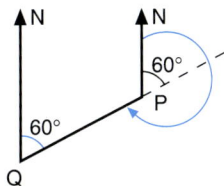

Bearing of Q from P
= 60° + 180°
= 240°

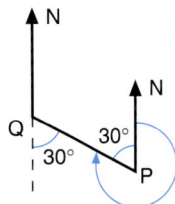

Bearing of Q from P
= 360° − 30°
= 330°

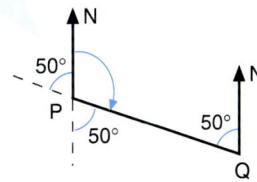

Bearing of Q from P
= 180° − 50°
= 130°

# Transformations

A **transformation** changes the **position** or **size** of a shape.

There are four types of transformations: translations, reflections, rotations and enlargements.

## Translations

These move figures from one place to another. The size and shape of the figure are not changed.

**Vectors** are used to describe the distance and direction of the translation.

A vector is written as $\begin{bmatrix} a \\ b \end{bmatrix}$. $a$ represents the **horizontal** movement,

and $b$ represents the **vertical** movement.

### Example

(a)  Translate ABC by the vector $\begin{bmatrix} 2 \\ 1 \end{bmatrix}$.

Call it P.

> This means 2 to the right and 1 upwards.

(b)  Translate ABC by the vector $\begin{bmatrix} -3 \\ -2 \end{bmatrix}$.

Call it Q.

> This means 3 to the left and 2 down.

P and Q are **congruent**.

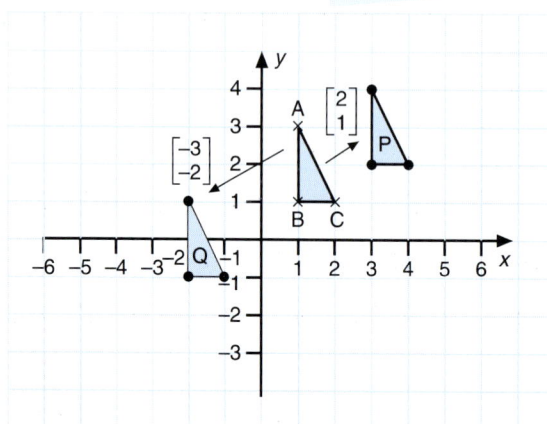

## Reflections

When describing reflections you must state where the mirror line is.

These create an image of an object on the other side of a *mirror line*. The mirror line is known as an **axis of reflection**. The size and shape of the figure are not changed.

## Example

Reflect triangle ABC in:

   (a)  the x axis, and call it D;

   (b)  the line y = −x, and call it E;

   (c)  the line x = 5, and call it F.

   D, E and F are congruent to triangle ABC.

> Count the squares of the object from the mirror. It's easier.

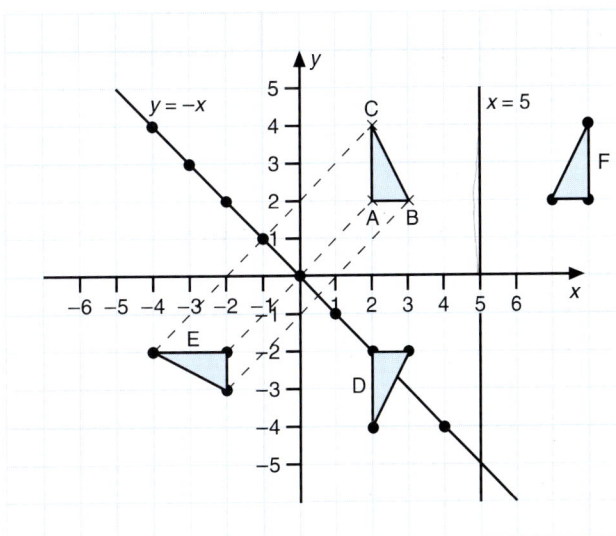

## Rotations

These **turn** a figure through an angle about some fixed point. This fixed point is called the **centre of rotation**. The size and shape of the figure are not changed.

## Example

Rotate triangle ABC:

   (a)  90° clockwise about (0, 0) and call it R;

   (b)  180° about (0, 0), and call it S;

   (c)  90° anticlockwise about (−1, 1), and call it T.

> Tracing paper can be used in the examination and is particularly useful when rotating shapes.

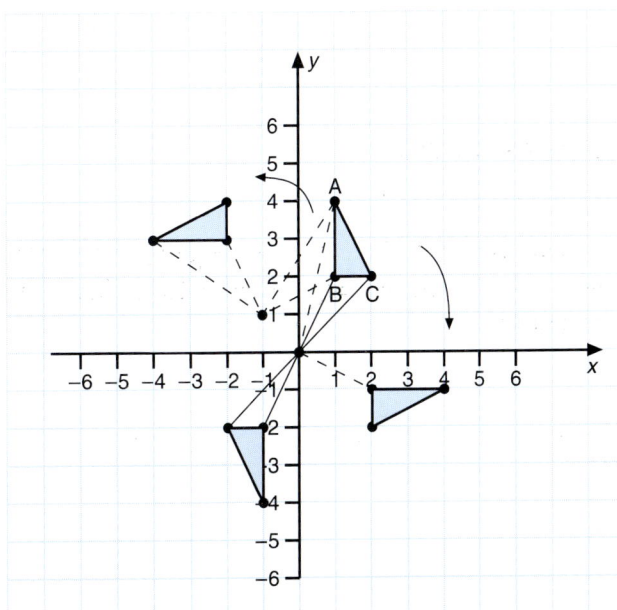

59

When describing a rotation, give:

- the **centre** of rotation;

- the **direction** of the turn (clockwise/anticlockwise);

- the **angle** of the turn.

## Enlargements

These change the size but not the shape of an object.

The **centre of enlargement** is the point from which the enlargement takes place. The **scale factor** indicates how many times the lengths of the original figure have changed size.

- If the scale factor is **greater than 1**, the shape becomes **bigger**.

- If the scale factor is **less than 1**, the shape becomes **smaller**.

### Example

Enlarge triangle ABC by a scale factor of 2, centre = (0, 0). Call it A'B'C'.

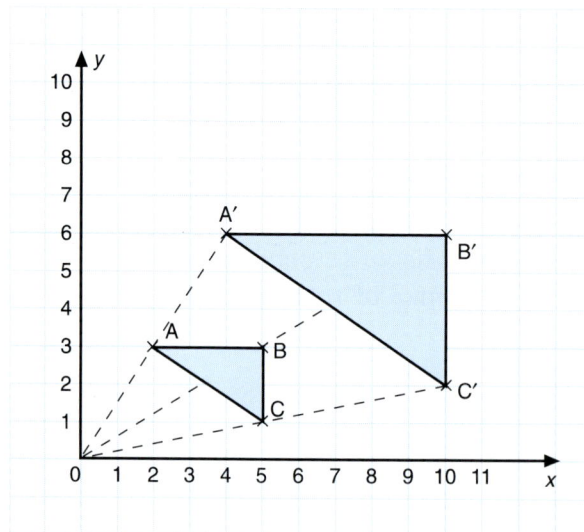

Notice each side of the enlargement is twice the size of the original.

OC' = 2OC.

### Example

Describe fully the transformation that maps ABCDEF onto A'B'C'D'E'F'.

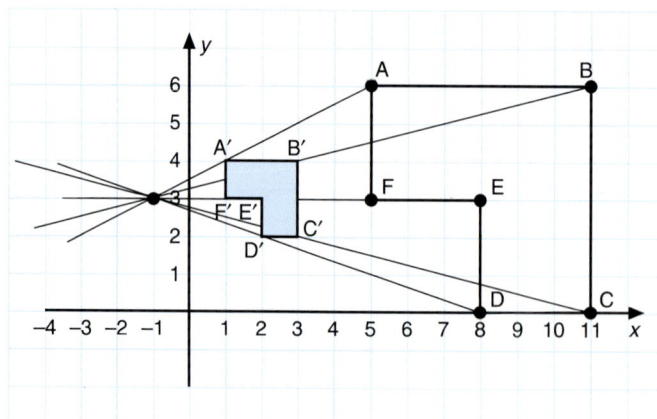

- To find the centre of enlargement, join A to A', and continue the line. Join B to B', and continue the line. Do the same for the others.

- Where all the lines meet is the centre of enlargement (−1, 3).

- The transformation is an enlargement with scale factor $\frac{1}{3}$. The centre of enlargement is at (−1, 3).

When asked to describe an enlargement you must include the scale factor and the position of the centre of enlargement.

## Combining transformations

These are a series of two or more transformations.

**Example**

For triangle ABC:

(a)  Reflect ABC in the x axis. Call the image $A_1B_1C_1$.

(b)  Reflect $A_1B_1C_1$ in the y axis. Call the image $A_2B_2C_2$.

The single transformation that maps ABC onto $A_2B_2C_2$ directly is a rotation of 180°, centre (0, 0).

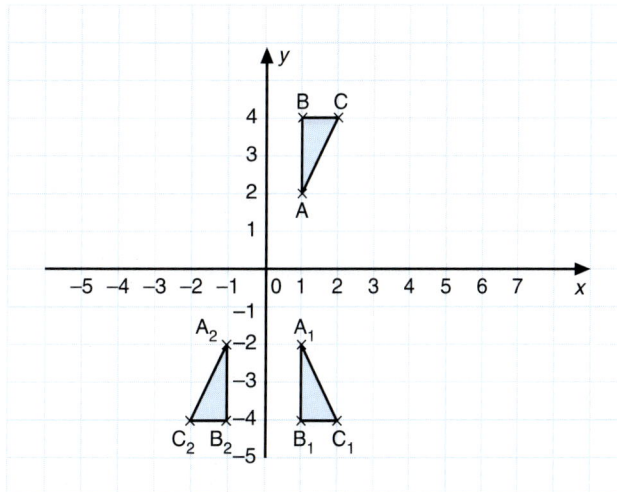

# Similarity

Similar figures are those which are the **same shape** but **different sizes**.

Corresponding angles are equal.

Corresponding lengths are in the same ratio.

**Examples**

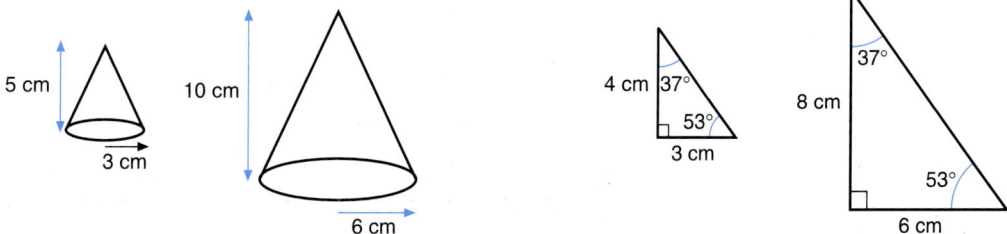

## Finding missing lengths of similar figures

### Example

Find the missing length $a$, giving your answer to 2 s.f.

9 cm

14 cm

$a$

11 cm

Make sure that all working out is shown.

$\dfrac{a}{11} = \dfrac{9}{14}$    Corresponding sides are in the same ratio.

$a = \dfrac{9}{14} \times 11$    Multiply both sides by 11.

$a = 7.1$ cm (2 s.f.)

### Example

Calculate the missing length.

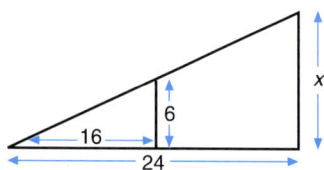

6

$x$

16

24

Measurements in cm

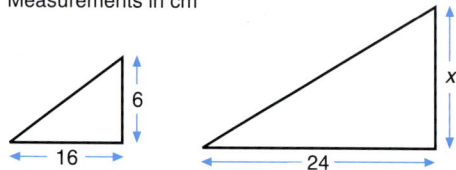

Don't forget that corresponding angles are equal.

6

16

$x$

24

It is useful to draw the two triangles first.

$\dfrac{x}{6} = \dfrac{24}{16}$    Corresponding sides are in the same ratio.

$x = \dfrac{24}{16} \times 6$    Multiply both sides by 6.

$x = 9$ cm

# Constructions

## The perpendicular bisector of a line

• Draw a line XY.

• Draw two arcs with the compasses, using X as the centre. The compasses must be set at a radius greater than half the distance of XY.

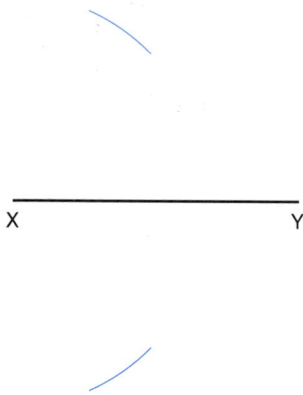

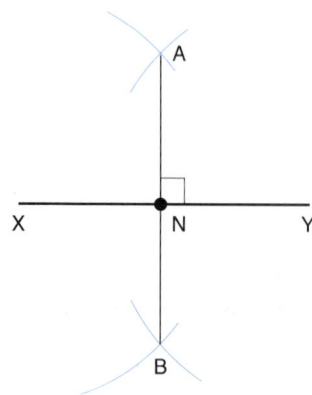

X                Y

A

X          N          Y

B

- Draw two more arcs with Y as the centre. (Keep the compasses the same distance apart as before.)
- Join the two points where the arcs cross.
- AB is the **perpendicular bisector** of XY.
- N is the **midpoint** of XY.

## Bisecting an angle

- Draw two lines XY and YZ to meet at an angle.
- Using compasses, place the point at Y and draw the two arcs on XY and YZ.
- Place the compass point at the two arcs on XY and YZ and draw arcs to cross at N. Join Y to N.

  YN is the **bisector** of angle XYZ.

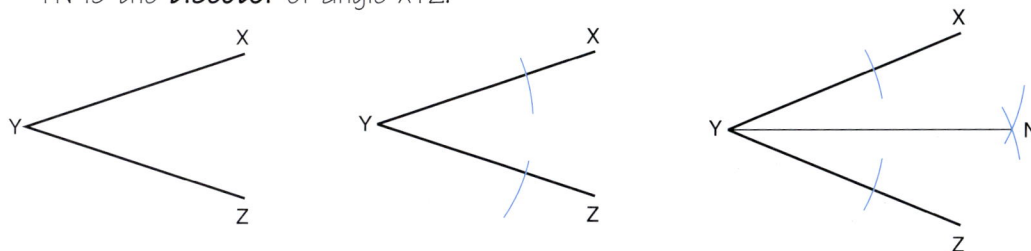

# Scale drawings

Scale drawings are very useful for measuring lengths which cannot be measured directly.

### Example

A ship sails from a harbour for 15 km on a bearing of 040°, and then continues due east for 20 km. Make a scale drawing of this journey using a scale of 1 cm to 5 km. How far will the ship have to sail to get back to the harbour by the shortest route? What will the bearing be?

Use a protractor to measure the angle and a ruler to measure the distance.

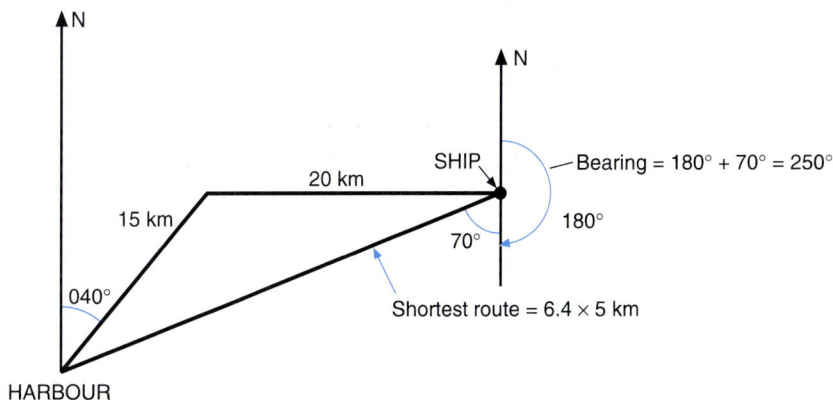

Shortest route = 6.4 × 5 km = 32 km

Bearing = 70° + 180° = 250°

## Maps

Scales are often used on maps. They are usually written as a ratio.

### Example

The scale on a road map is 1 : 25 000. Bury and Oldham are 20 cm apart on the map. Work out the real distance, in km, between Bury and Oldham.

Scale 1 : 25 000, distance on map is 20 cm.

   Real distance = 20 × 25 000 = 500 000 cm

Divide by 100 to change cm to m.

   500 000 ÷ 100 = 5000 m

Divide by 1000 to change m to km.

   5000 ÷ 1000 = 5 km

> A scale of 1 : 25 000 means that 1 cm on the scale drawing represents a real length of 25 000 cm.

# Locus

The **locus** of a point is the set of all the possible positions which that point can occupy, subject to some given condition or rule.

The plural of locus is **loci**.

## Common loci

The locus of the points which are a constant distance from a fixed point is a circle.

The locus of the points which are equidistant from two points XY is the perpendicular bisector of XY.

> You need to learn how to do the above constructions before you can do loci accurately.

The locus of the points which are equidistant from two lines is the line which bisects the angle.

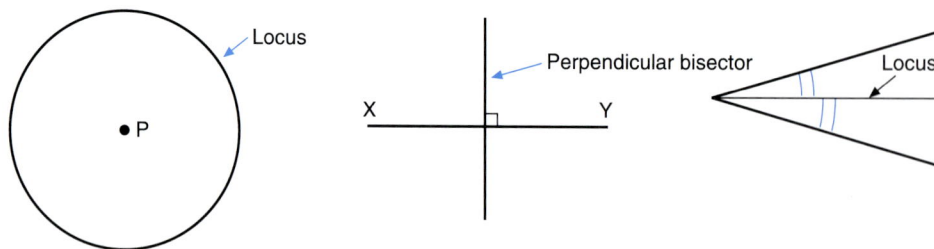

The locus of the points which are a constant distance from a line XY is a pair of parallel lines above and below XY.

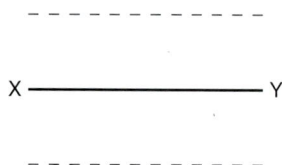

> Draw the locus carefully and measure accurately.

## Example

A new hospital (H) is being built so that it is equidistant from the train station and the gas depot. The hospital cannot be within 80 m of the gas depot in case of a leak. Using a scale of 1 cm to 20 m, show the first available position for where the hospital can be built.

- Construct the perpendicular bisector between the train station and the gas depot.

- Draw a circle of radius 4 cm since nothing can be built within 80 m of the depot.

- The hospital (H) is shown.

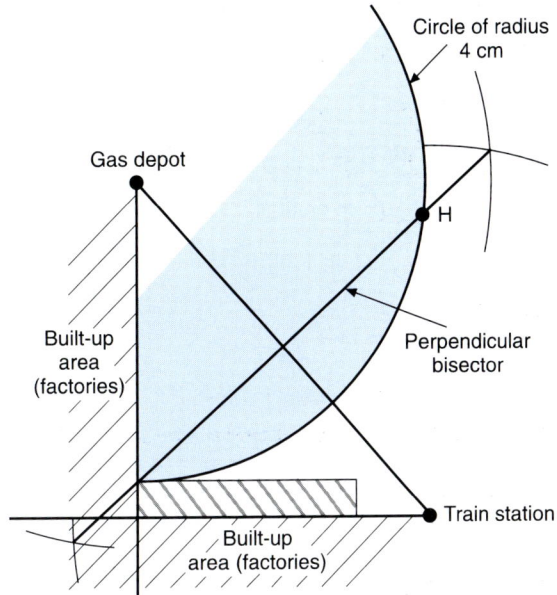

# Questions

1 Explain why a regular heptagon will not tessellate.

2 What are the bearings of A from B in the following?

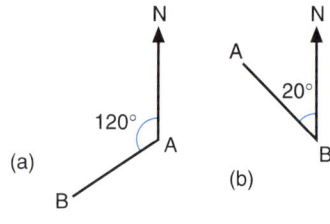

3 What does the vector $\begin{bmatrix} -2 \\ 3 \end{bmatrix}$ mean?

(a)

(b)

4 On the diagram on the right:

(a) Translate ABC by the vector $\begin{bmatrix} -3 \\ 1 \end{bmatrix}$. Call it P.

(b) Reflect ABC in the line y = x. Call it Q.

(c) Reflect ABC in the line y = −1. Call it R.

(d) Rotate ABC 180° about (0, 0). Call it S.

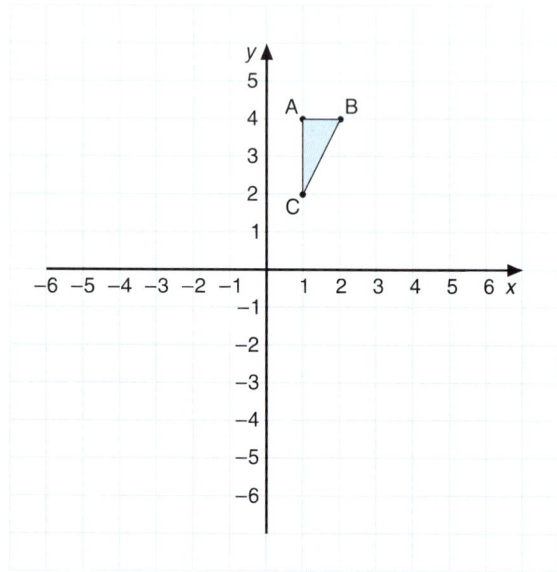

5 Draw an enlargement of shape P with a scale factor of 2, centre of enlargement as shown.

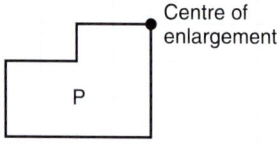

Centre of enlargement

P

6 Bisect this angle.

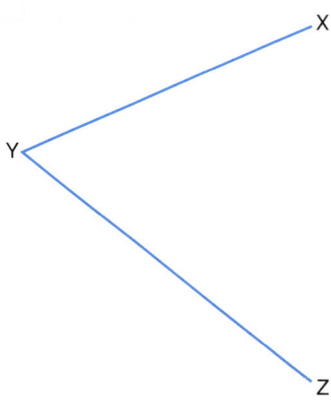

X

Y

Z

7 Find the lengths labelled by letters in these similar shapes.

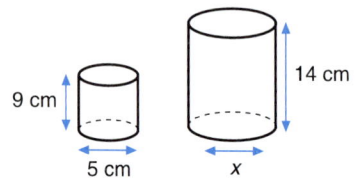

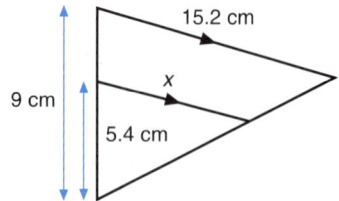

9 cm    14 cm

5 cm    x

(a)

15.2 cm

9 cm    x

5.4 cm

(b)

# Measures

## Units

### Metric units

| Length | Weight | Capacity |
|---|---|---|
| 10 mm = 1 cm | 1000 mg = 1 g | 1000 ml = 1 l |
| 100 cm = 1 m | 1000 g = 1 kg | 100 cl = 1 l |
| 1000 m = 1 km | 1000 kg = 1 tonne | 1000 $cm^3$ = 1 l |

### Converting units

- If changing from **small** units to **large** units (for example, g to kg), **divide**.

- If changing from **large** units to **small** units (for example, km to m), **multiply**.

**Examples**

(a)  Change 50 mm into cm.

mm are smaller than cm, so
divide by the number of mm in a cm.

50 ÷ 10 = 5 cm.

(b)  Change 6 km into mm.

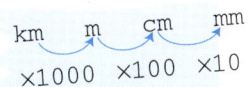

km are bigger than mm, so
multiply by the number of m in a km,
cm in a m and mm in a cm.

$$km \xrightarrow{\times 1000} m \xrightarrow{\times 100} cm \xrightarrow{\times 10} mm$$

6 × 1000 × 100 × 10 = 6 000 000 mm.

### Imperial units

| Length | Weight | Capacity |
|---|---|---|
| 1 foot = 12 inches | 1 stone = 14 pounds (lb) | 20 fluid oz = 1 pint |
| 1 yard = 3 feet | 1 pound = 16 ounces (oz) | 8 pints = 1 gallon |

**Examples**

(a)  Change 4 yards into inches.

Change yards to feet (× 3) and feet to inches (× 12).

4 × 3 × 12 = 144 inches.

(b)  Change 166 pints into gallons.

8 pints = 1 gallon, so 1 pint = $\frac{1}{8}$ gallon.

166 ÷ 8 = 20.75 gallons.

## Comparisons between metric and imperial units

The conversions marked with * need to be learnt.

| Length | Weight | Capacity |
|---|---|---|
| 2.5 cm ≈ 1 inch | 25 g ≈ 1 ounce | *1 litre ≈ $1\frac{3}{4}$ pints |
| *30 cm ≈ 1 foot | *1 kg ≈ 2.2 pounds | *4.5 litres ≈ 1 gallon |
| *1 m ≈ 39 inches | | |
| *8 km ≈ 5 miles | | |

Some of the comparisons between metric and imperial units are only approximate.

**Example**

Change 25 km into miles.

8 km ≈ 5 miles.

1 km ≈ $\frac{5}{8}$ mile = 0.625 miles.

25 km ≈ 25 × 0.625 = 15.625 miles.

> Check that the answer seems sensible.

# Accuracy of measurement

There are two types of measurements: discrete measurements and continuous measurements.

## Discrete measures

These are quantities that can be counted; for example, the number of baked bean tins on a shelf.

## Continuous measures

These are measurements which have been made by using a measuring instrument; for example, the height of a person.

Continuous measures are **not exact**.

**Example**

Nigel weighs 72 kg to the nearest kg. His actual weight could be anywhere between 71.5 kg and 72.5 kg.

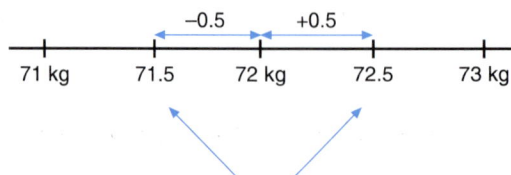

These two values are the **limits** of Nigel's weight.

If W represents weight, then

$$71.5 \leq W < 72.5$$

This is the **lower limit** of Nigel's weight (sometimes known as the **lower bound**). Anything below 71.5 would be recorded as 71 kg.

This is the **upper limit** (**upper bound**) of Nigel's weight. Anything from 72.5 upwards would be recorded as 73 kg.

### Example

The length of a seedling is measured as 3.7 cm to the nearest tenth of a cm. What are the upper and lower limits of the length?

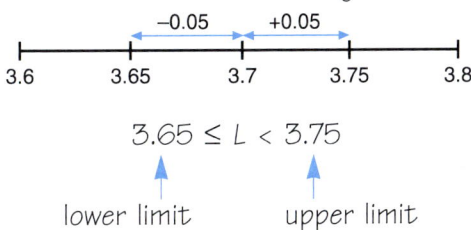

−0.05    +0.05

3.6    3.65    3.7    3.75    3.8

$$3.65 \leq L < 3.75$$

lower limit    upper limit

Remember that the measurement cannot be equal to the upper limit.

In general, if a measurement is accurate to some given amount, then the true value lies within a maximum of a half a unit of that amount.

# Areas and volumes

**Perimeter** – This is the distance around the outside edge of a shape.

**Area** – This is the amount of space a 2D shape covers. Common units of area are mm$^2$, cm$^2$, m$^2$, etc.

**Volume** – This is the amount of space a 3D shape occupies. Common units of volume are mm$^3$, cm$^3$, m$^3$, etc.

## Areas of quadrilaterals and triangles

### Area of a rectangle

W, L

Area = length × width
$A = L \times W$

### Area of a parallelogram

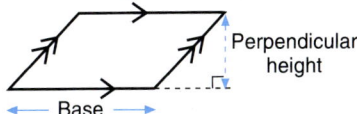

Perpendicular height, Base

Area = base × perpendicular height
$A = b \times h$

Use letters to write the formulae. It's quicker!

### Area of a triangle

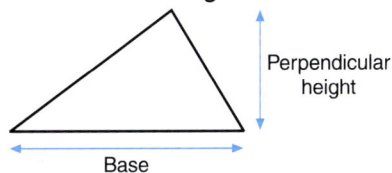

Perpendicular height, Base

Area = $\frac{1}{2}$ × base × perpendicular height
$A = \frac{1}{2} \times b \times h$

### Area of a trapezium

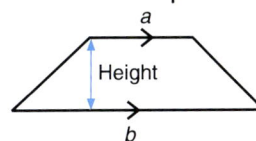

a, Height, b

Area = $\frac{1}{2}$ × (sum of parallel sides) × perpendicular height between them
$A = \frac{1}{2} \times (a + b) \times h$

### Examples

Find the areas of the following shapes, giving the answers to 3 s.f. where necessary.

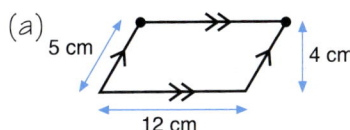

Check that you write the correct units at the end of the question.

(a) 5 cm, 4 cm, 12 cm

$A = b \times h$
$= 12 \times 4$
$= 48$ cm$^2$

Remember to use the perpendicular height, not the slant height.

(b)

$A = \frac{1}{2} \times (a + b) \times h$

$= \frac{1}{2} \times (4.9 + 10.1) \times 6.2$

$= 46.5 \text{ cm}^2$

4.9 cm    10.1 cm    6.2 cm

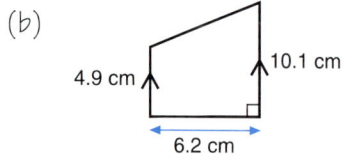

(c)

① 4.7 cm
② 5.5 cm
12.3 cm

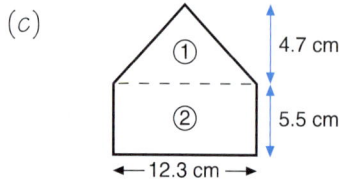

Split the shape into two parts and find the area of each.

Area of ① $= \frac{1}{2} \times b \times h$

$= \frac{1}{2} \times 12.3 \times 4.7$

$= 28.905 \text{ cm}^2$

Area of ② $= b \times h$

$= 12.3 \times 5.5$

$= 67.65 \text{ cm}^2$

Now find the total area by adding the two parts together.

Total area $=$ ① $+$ ②

$= 28.905 + 67.65$

$= 96.555$

$= 96.6 \text{ cm}^3$ (3 s.f.)

### Example

If the area of this triangle is 55 cm², find the height, giving your answer to 3 s.f.

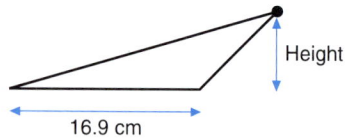

$A = \frac{1}{2} \times b \times h$

$55 = \frac{1}{2} \times 16.9 \times h$     Substitute the values into the formula.

$55 = 8.45 \times h$     Divide both sides by 8.45.

$\frac{55}{8.45} = h$     So $h = 6.51$ cm (to 3 s.f.)

Height

16.9 cm

## Circumference and area of a circle

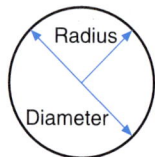

Radius
Diameter

circumference $= \pi \times$ diameter     $C = \pi \times d$

$= 2 \times \pi \times$ radius     $= 2 \times \pi \times r$

area     $= \pi \times (\text{radius})^2$     $A = \pi \times r^2$

### Example

The diameter of a circular rose garden is 5 m.
Find the circumference and area of the rose garden.

5 m

$C = \pi \times d$     Substitute in the formula.

$= 3.14 \times 5$     Use $\pi = 3.14$ or the value of $\pi$ on your calculator.

$= 15.7$ m     EXP often gives the value of $\pi$.

When finding the area, work out the radius first.

$d = 2 \times r$ so $r = d \div 2$, and $r = 2.5$ cm

$A = \pi \times r^2$

$= 3.14 \times 2.5^2$     Remember $2.5^2$ means $2.5 \times 2.5$.

$= 19.625$

$= 19.6 \text{ m}^2$ (3 s.f.)

## Example

A circle has an area of 40 cm². Find the radius of the circle, giving your answer to 3 s.f. Use $\pi = 3.14$.

$A = \pi \times r^2$

$40 = 3.14 \times r^2$          Substitute the values into the formula.

$\dfrac{40}{3.14} = r^2$          Divide both sides by 3.14.

$r^2 = 12.738\ldots$

$r = \sqrt{12.738}\ldots$          Take the square root to find r.

$= 3.57$ cm (3 s.f.)

> You must use the value of $\pi$ which the question tells you to use.

# Volumes of 3D shapes

### Volume of a cuboid

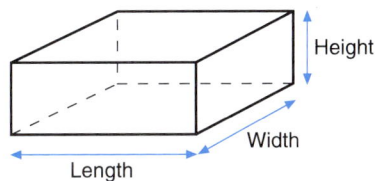

### Volume of a prism

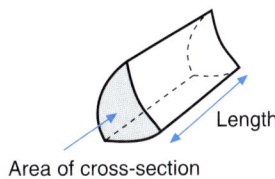

Area of cross-section

> A **prism** is any solid which can be cut into slices, which are all the same shape. This is called having a **uniform cross-section**.

volume = length × width × height
$V = l \times w \times h$

volume = area of cross-section × length
$V = a \times l$

### Volume of a cylinder

Cylinders are prisms where the cross-section is a circle.

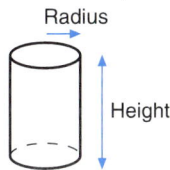

volume = area of cross-section × length

$$V = \pi r^2 \times h$$

area of circle       height or length

### Examples

Find the volumes of the following 3D shapes, giving the answer to 3 s.f. Use $\pi = 3.14$.

(a)

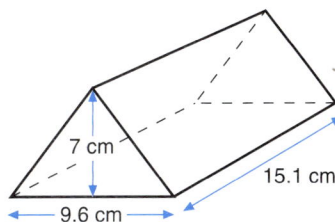

7 cm      15.1 cm

9.6 cm

(b)   10.7 cm

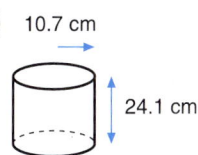

24.1 cm

> Remember to divide by 2 when working out the area of a triangle.

$V = a \times l$

$= (\tfrac{1}{2} \times b \times h) \times l$

$= (\tfrac{1}{2} \times 9.6 \times 7) \times 15.1$

$= 507.36$ cm³

$= 507$ cm³ (3 s.f.)

> The area of cross-section is the area of a triangle.

$V = \pi r^2 \times h$

$= 3.14 \times 10.7^2 \times 24.1$

$= 8663.92$ cm³

$= 8660$ cm³ (3 s.f.)

## Example

If the volume of the cylinder is 500 cm³, work out the radius. Use $\pi$ = 3.14.

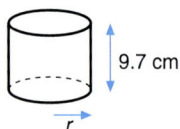

9.7 cm

$r$

$V = \pi r^2 \times h$

Work this question out slowly, showing each step in your working.

$500 = 3.14 \times r^2 \times 9.7$      Substitute into the formula.

$500 = 30.458 \times r^2$

$\dfrac{500}{30.458} = r^2$      Divide both sides by 30.458

$r^2 = 16.416 \ldots$      Take the square root to find the radius.

$r = \sqrt{16.416 \ldots}$      So $r = 4.05$ cm (3 s.f.)

# Dimensions

- The dimension of **perimeter** is length (L); it is a measurement in *one* dimension.

- The dimension of **area** is length × length (L × L = L²); it is a measurement in *two* dimensions.

- The dimension of **volume** is length × length × length (L × L × L = L³); it is a measurement in *three* dimensions.

- Values like $\frac{4}{3}$, $\pi$, 6.2, etc have no dimensions.

## Examples

The letters *a*, *b*, *c* and *d* all represent lengths. For each expression, write down whether it represents a length, area or volume.

Adding two lots of area together has no effect – it's still area.

(a)   $a^2 + b^2$ = (length × length) + (length × length) = area

$L^2 + L^2$

A formula with a mixed dimension is impossible.

(b)   $\frac{1}{3} \pi abc$ = number × length × length × length = volume

$L^3$

(c)   $2\pi a + \frac{3}{4}\pi d$ = (number × length) + (number × length) = length

$L + L$

(d)   $\frac{5}{9}\pi a^2 d + \pi b^2 c^2$ = (number × length × length × length) + (number × length² × length²) = none

$L^3 + L^4$

A dimension greater than 3 is impossible, so it has no dimension.

## Measures
# Questions

1 Change 3500 g into kg.

2 Change 3 stone into pounds.

3 Change 6 litres into pints.

4 Write down the upper and lower limits for a time of 9.2 seconds, rounded to the nearest tenth of a second.

5 Work out the area of the following shapes, giving your answers to 3 s.f.

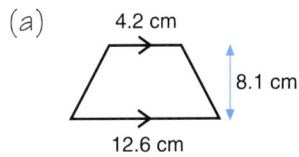

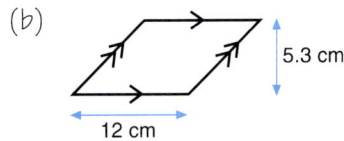

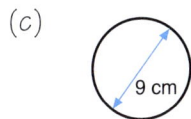

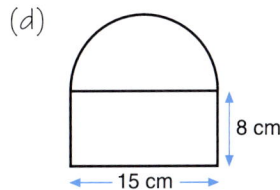

(a)

4.2 cm

8.1 cm

12.6 cm

(b)

5.3 cm

12 cm

(c)

9 cm

(d)

8 cm

15 cm

6 Work out the volume of the following 3D shapes. Give your answer to 3 s.f.

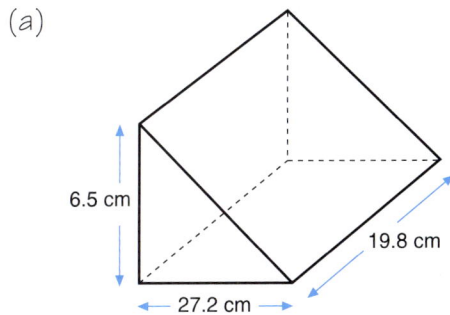

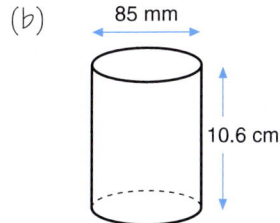

(a)

6.5 cm

19.8 cm

27.2 cm

(b)

85 mm

10.6 cm

7 The volume of a cylinder is 2000 cm$^3$ and the radius is 5.6 cm. Work out the height to 3 s.f.

8 $x$, $y$, $z$ represent lengths. For each expression write down whether it could represent perimeter, area or volume.

(a) $\sqrt{x^2 + y^2 + z^2}$

(b) $\frac{5}{9}\pi x^3 + 2y^3$

(c) $\frac{1}{3}\frac{xyz^2}{y}$

(d) $\frac{9}{5}\pi xy + \frac{4}{5}\pi yz$

# Handling data

## Types of data

- **Quantitative** – The answer is a **number**; e.g. how many red cars are in the car park?

- **Qualitative** – The answer is a **word**; e.g. what is your favourite colour?

- **Discrete data** – Each category is separate. It is often found by counting. Examples include the number of people with blue eyes.

- **Continuous data** – Here the values change from one category to the next. Such data is often found by measuring. Examples include heights and weights of Year 9 pupils.

# Hypotheses, experiments and questionnaires

A **hypothesis** is a prediction which can be tested.

## Experiments

Experiments are used to test hypotheses. They may contain several variables.

**Example**

**Hypothesis** – 'The better the light, the more the seedlings grow.'

**Variable** – This is the intensity of the light which will be changed.

**Conditions** – The other conditions must stay the same. All seedlings must be exactly the same size, strength and colour. If there is **bias** (e.g. one side of the tray gets extra sunlight) then the experiment has to start again.

## Questionnaires

Questionnaires can be used to test hypotheses.

When designing questionnaires:

- Decide what needs to be found out, the 'hypotheses'.

- Give instructions on how the questionnaire has to be filled in.

- Do not ask for information which is not needed (e.g. name).

- Make the questions clear and concise.

Word any questions you write very carefully.

- Keep the questionnaire short.

- If people's opinion is needed, make sure the question is **unbiased**. An example of a biased question would be: 'Do you agree that a leisure centre should have a tennis court rather than a squash court?'

- Allow for any possible answers — for example:

  How many hours (to the nearest hour) a day do you watch TV?

  0–2 ☐   3–5 ☐   6–8 ☐   More than 8 ☐

# Pie charts

These are used to illustrate data. They are circles split into sections, each section representing a certain number of items.

## Calculating angles for a pie chart

- Find the total for the items listed.

- Find the fraction of the total for each item.

- Multiply the fraction by 360° to find the angle.

### Example

The hair colour of 24 ten-year-olds:

| Hair colour | Frequency |
|---|---|
| Brown | 8 |
| Auburn | 4 |
| Blonde | 6 |
| Black | 6 |
| | Total = 24 |

Key in on the calculator

8 ÷ 24 × 360 =

**Finding the angle**

Brown $= \frac{8}{24} \times 360° = 120°$

Auburn $= \frac{4}{24} \times 360° = 60°$

Blonde $= \frac{6}{24} \times 360° = 90°$

Black $= \frac{6}{24} \times 360° = 90°$

Total $= 360°$

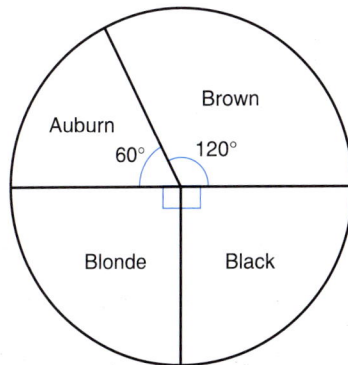

Check that the angles add up to 360°.

## Interpreting pie charts

**Example**

The pie chart shows the number of pupils choosing different options. If 48 choose Art, how many choose Technology?

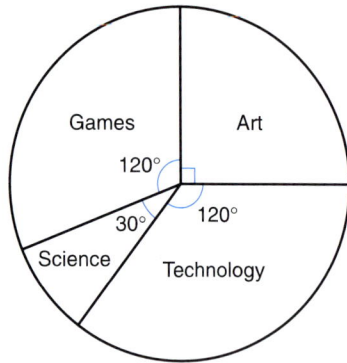

90° represents 48 pupils

1° represents $\frac{48}{90} = 0.5\dot{3}\dot{3}$ pupils

Technology $= 120 \times 0.5\dot{3}\dot{3} = 64$ pupils

(120 lots of $0.5\dot{3}\dot{3}$)

Check that your answers seem sensible.

Make sure that this number is not rounded off!

# Line graphs

These are a set of points joined by lines.

| Year | 1988 | 1989 | 1990 | 1991 | 1992 | 1993 |
|---|---|---|---|---|---|---|
| Number of cars sold | 2500 | 2900 | 2100 | 1900 | 1600 | 800 |

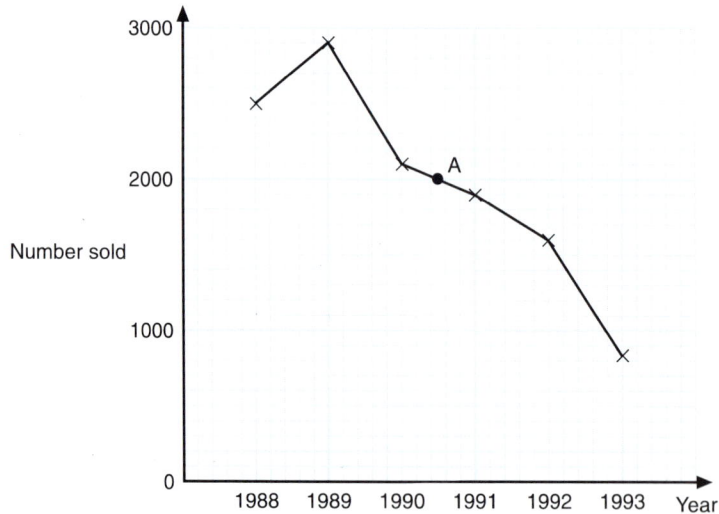

**Middle values**, like point A, have no meaning. A does **not** mean that halfway between 1990 and 1991, there were 2000 cars sold.

# Histograms

These are drawn to illustrate **continuous data**. They are similar to bar charts except there are no gaps between the bars. The data must be grouped into **equal** class intervals if the length of the bar is used to represent the frequency.

**Example**

The weights of 30 workers in a factory are shown in the table.

| Weight (kg) | Frequency |
|---|---|
| $45 \leq w < 55$ | 7 |
| $55 \leq w < 65$ | 13 |
| $65 \leq w < 75$ | 6 |
| $75 \leq w < 85$ | 4 |
| | 30 |

$45 \leq w < 55$, etc. are called **class intervals** – they are all equal in width.

$55 \leq w < 65$ means the weights are between 55 kg and 65 kg.

$55 \leq$ means that $w$ can be equal to 55 kg, while
$< 65$ means that $w$ cannot be equal to 65 kg (it would be in the next group).

Note:

- The axes do not need to start at zero.

- The axes are labelled.

- The graph has a title.

If the scale on either axis doesn't start at zero then attention should be drawn to this fact by using a jagged line like

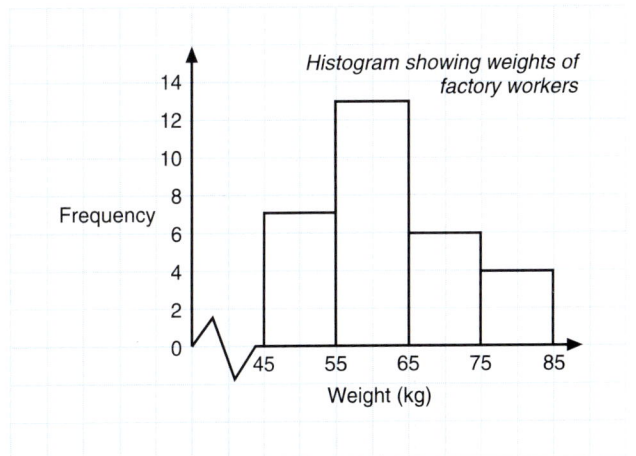

Histogram showing weights of factory workers

# Frequency polygons

These are used to join the **midpoints of class intervals** for grouped or continuous data.

Consider the histogram of the factory workers again.

For a frequency polygon remember to plot at the midpoints of the class intervals.

A frequency polygon is said to show the **trend** of the data.

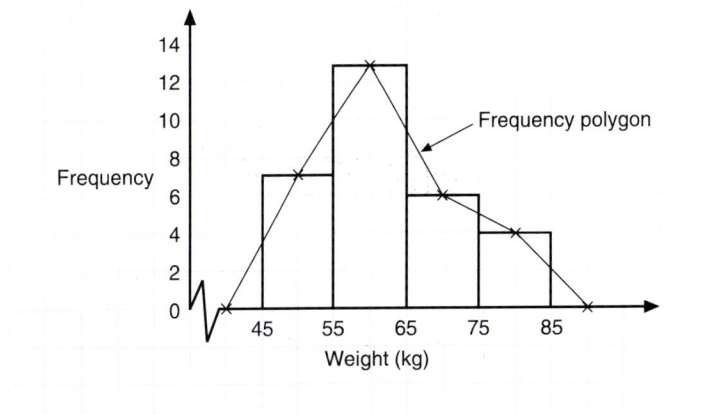

Frequency polygon

To draw the frequency polygon:

- Put a cross on the middle of each bar.

- Join the crosses up with a ruler.

- Draw the line from the midpoint on the first bar to the x axis which is half a class interval before the first bar.

- Draw the line from the midpoint on the last bar to the x axis which is half a class interval after the last bar.

# Scatter diagrams

A scatter diagram (scatter graph or scatter plot) is used to show two sets of data at the same time.

Its importance is to show the **correlation** (connection) between two sets of data. There are three types of correlation: positive, negative or zero.

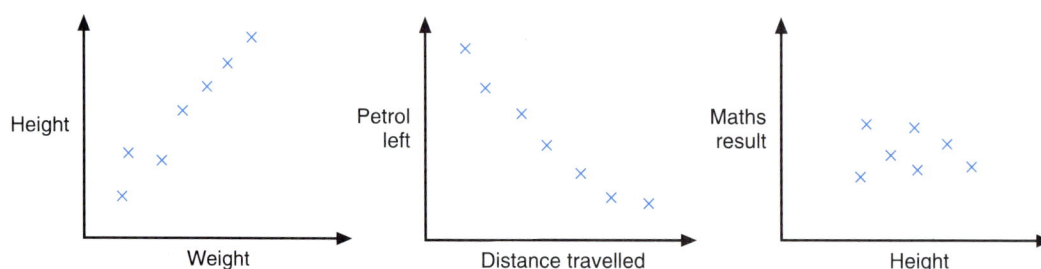

**Positive** – This is when both variables are increasing. If the points are nearly a straight line it is said to have a **high positive correlation**.

**Negative** – This is when one variable increases whilst the other decreases. The one above has a **high negative correlation**.

**Zero** – This is when there is little or no correlation between the variables.

## Drawing a scatter diagram

- Work out the scales first.

- Plot the points carefully.

- Each time a point is plotted, tick them off.

Do not rush when drawing a scatter diagram, otherwise you will plot the points incorrectly.

**Example**

| Maths test (%) | 64 | 79 | 38 | 42 | 49 | 75 | 83 | 82 | 66 | 61 | 54 |
|---|---|---|---|---|---|---|---|---|---|---|---|
| History test (%) | 70 | 36 | 84 | 70 | 74 | 42 | 29 | 33 | 50 | 56 | 64 |

The table shows the maths and history results of 11 pupils.

The scatter diagram overleaf shows there is a **strong negative correlation** – in general, the better the pupils did in maths, the worse they did in history, and vice versa.

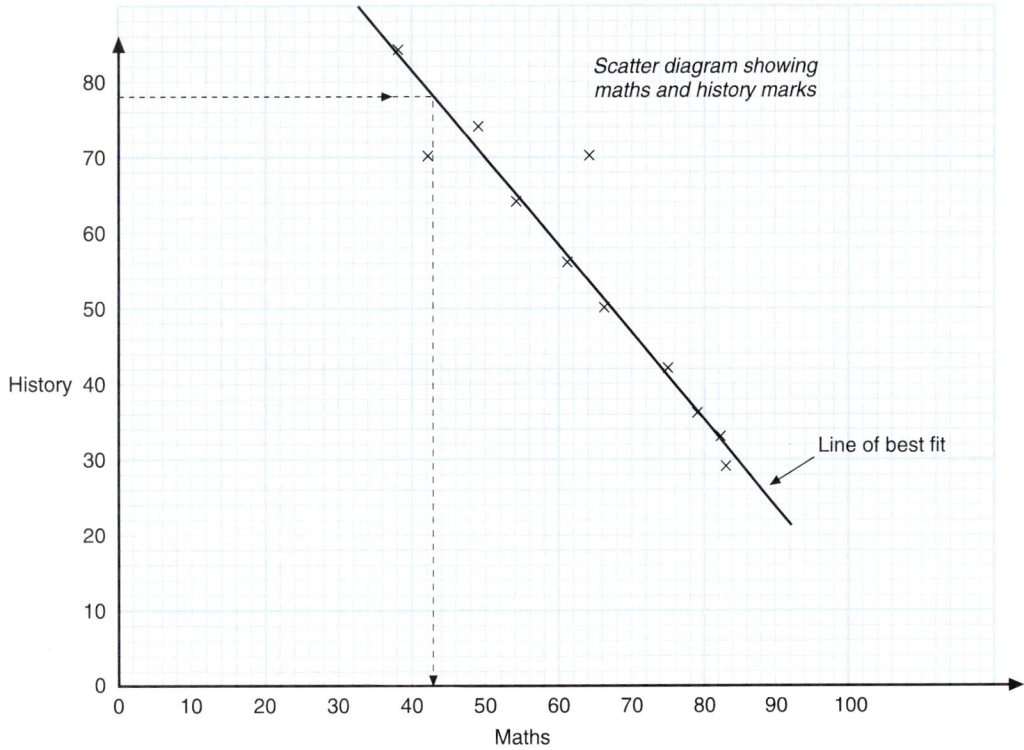

*Scatter diagram showing maths and history marks*

Line of best fit

## Line of best fit

This is the line which best fits the data. It goes in the direction of the data and has roughly the same number of points above the line as below it.

A line of best fit can be used to make predictions.

*Draw your line in pencil carefully.*

### Example

Amy was away for the maths test. If she got 78% in history, estimate what she would have obtained for maths.

Go to 78% on history scale. Read across to the line, then down. The estimate is approximately 44% in maths.

# Averages and range

There are three types of averages: mean, median and mode.

$$\text{Mean} = \frac{\text{Sum of a set of values}}{\text{The number of values used}}$$

**Median** – The middle value when the numbers are put in order of size.

**Mode** – The one that occurs the most often.

**Range** – This tells us the spread of information.

Range = highest value – lowest value.

### Example

Find the mean, median, mode and range of: 2, 9, 3, 6, 4, 4, 5, 8, 4.

$$\text{Mean} = \frac{2 + 9 + 3 + 6 + 4 + 4 + 5 + 8 + 4}{9} = \frac{45}{9} = 5$$

Median        2, 3, 4, 4, 4, 5, 6, 8, 9        Put in order of size.

2̸, 3̸, 4̸, 4̸, ④, 5̸, 6̸, 8̸, 9̸        Cross off from the end to find the middle.

Median = 4

> If there are two numbers in the middle the median is halfway between them.

Mode = 4 as it occurs 3 times.

Range = 9 − 2 = 7

> Remember to subtract the two values in order to obtain the range.

# Finding averages from a frequency table

A frequency table just tells us **how many** are in a group.

> this means that 2 people had 4 sisters

**Example**

| Number of sisters (x) | 0 | 1 | 2 | 3 | 4 | 5 |
|---|---|---|---|---|---|---|
| Frequency (f) | 4 | 9 | 3 | 5 | 2 | 0 |

## Mean

$$\bar{x} = \frac{\Sigma fx}{\Sigma f} = \frac{\text{total of results when multiplied}}{\text{total of frequency}}$$

> $\Sigma$ means 'the sum of'.

$$= \frac{(4 \times 0) + (9 \times 1) + (3 \times 2) + (5 \times 3) + (2 \times 4) + (0 \times 5)}{4 + 9 + 3 + 5 + 2 + 0}$$

$$= \frac{38}{23} = 1.65 \text{ (2 d.p.)}$$

> You must remember to divide by the sum of the **frequency**.

## Median

Add up the frequencies: 4 + 9 + 3 + 5 + 2 = 23

The median will be the 12th person _____ 12 _____

                                    11 people              11 people

4 + 9 = 13 people so the 12th person has 1 sister. Median = 1.

## Mode

> For the mode, remember to write down the answer 1, not the number 9 (this is the frequency).

This is the one with the highest frequency, that is 1 sister.

## Range

5 − 0 = 5 sisters

# Averages of grouped data

## Mean

When the data are grouped the exact data are not known. **Estimate** the mean by using the **midpoint** of the **class interval**. The midpoint is the halfway value.

### Example

The heights of year 10 pupils are shown in the table.

| Height (cm) | Frequency | Midpoint (x) |
|---|---|---|
| $140 \leq h < 145$ | 4 | 142.5 |
| $145 \leq h < 150$ | 7 | 147.5 |
| $150 \leq h < 155$ | 14 | 152.5 |
| $155 \leq h < 160$ | 5 | 157.5 |
| $160 \leq h < 165$ | 2 | 162.5 |

This is now the same as before except you multiply frequency by the midpoint.

If your calculator will do statistics, learn how to use it. It's much quicker, but do it twice to check.

$$\bar{x} = \frac{\sum fx}{\sum f} = \frac{(4 \times 142.5) + (7 \times 147.5) + (14 \times 152.5) + (5 \times 157.5) + (2 \times 162.5)}{4 + 7 + 14 + 5 + 2}$$

$$= \frac{4850}{32} = 151.56 \text{ cm (2 d.p.)}$$

## Mode

When using grouped (continuous) data only the **modal class** can be found. This is the one with the highest frequency.

For the year 10 height data,

the modal class is $150 \leq h < 155$

# Using appropriate averages

The **mean** is useful when a 'typical' value is wanted. Be careful not to use the mean if there are extreme values.

The **median** is a useful average to use if there are extreme values.

The **mode** is useful when the most common value is needed.

# Cumulative frequency diagrams

These are useful for finding the **median** and the **spread** of grouped data.

Before drawing the graph a cumulative frequency column on the table needs to be added.

### Example

The table shows the time in minutes for 49 pupils' journey times to school.

Remember to add the frequencies in order to get the cumulative frequencies.

| Time (in minutes) | Frequency | | Cumulative frequency | Time |
|---|---|---|---|---|
| $0 \leq t < 10$ | 15 | | 15 | <10 |
| $10 \leq t < 20$ | 16 | 15 + 16 | 31 | <20 |
| $20 \leq t < 30$ | 9 | 31 + 9 | 40 | <30 |
| $30 \leq t < 40$ | 6 | 40 + 6 | 46 | <40 |
| $40 \leq t < 50$ | 3 | 46 + 3 | 49 | <50 |

- Add up successive frequencies to get the cumulative frequency column.

We use the upper class boundaries.

- Plot (10, 15), (20, 31), (30, 40), etc.

- Since no people were less than zero time, the graph starts at (0, 0).

- Join the points with lines.

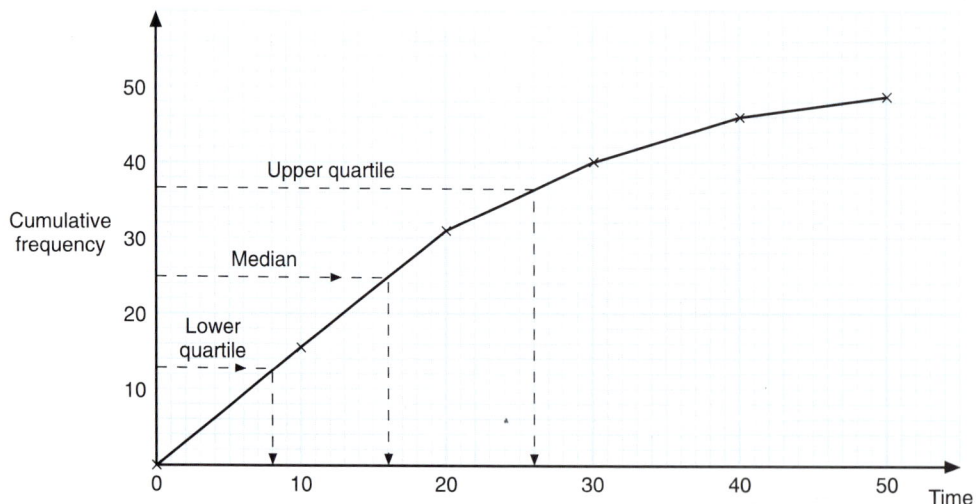

## Finding the median

The median is the **middle** value of the distribution.

For the journey time data,

Make sure your method is clearly shown on the graph.

median $= \frac{1}{2} \times$ total cumulative frequency $= \frac{1}{2} \times 49 = 24.5$

Read across then down. This shows median = 16 minutes.

## Finding the interquartile range

On nearly every cumulative frequency question you will be asked to find the median and/or interquartile range.

Interquartile range = upper quartile − lower quartile.

**Upper quartile** − This is the value **three-quarters** of the way into the distribution, that is at $\frac{3}{4} \times 49 = 36.75$

**Lower quartile** − This is the value **one-quarter** of the way into the distribution, that is at $\frac{1}{4} \times 49 = 12.25$

Read across the graph at the appropriate places.

upper quartile = 25.8

lower quartile = 8

interquartile range = 25.8 − 8 = 17.8

## Using the interquartile range

A large interquartile range indicates that much of the data is widely spread about the median.

A small interquartile range indicates that much of the data is concentrated about the median.

# Using averages and spread to compare distributions

Be careful when drawing conclusions from averages.

### Example

In a test, the boys got 16 as an average, but the girls got $17\frac{1}{2}$ as an average.

It seems that the girls did better, but on looking at the results:

Boys:  22, 22, 20, 0

Girls:  15, 20, 15, 20

It seems that half of the boys scored better marks than the girls.

### Example

|            | Median age | Interquartile range |
|------------|------------|---------------------|
| Village A  | 36         | 25                  |
| Village B  | 48         | 6                   |

From the table it appears that people in village B are older than village A.

However, the interquartile range for village A is much **bigger** and so it could be that village A has people who are as old or older than village B.

# Questions

1 (a) Using the histogram, complete the frequency table below.

| Height (cm) | Frequency |
|---|---|
| $140 \leq h < 145$ | |
| $145 \leq h < 150$ | 10 |
| $150 \leq h < 155$ | |
| $155 \leq h < 160$ | |
| $160 \leq h < 165$ | |

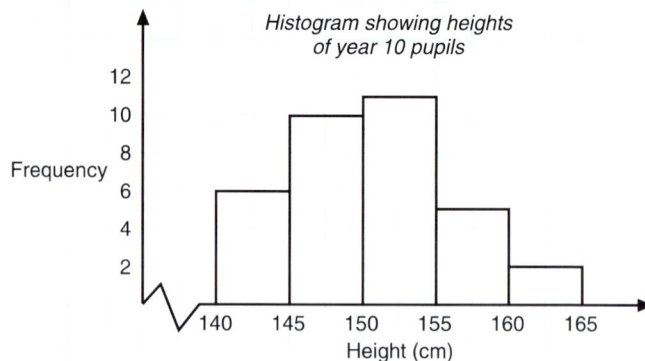

Histogram showing heights of year 10 pupils

(b) How many people were in the survey?

(c) Draw a frequency polygon on the histogram.

2 (a) Describe the correlation of the scatter diagram.

(b) Draw on the line of best fit.

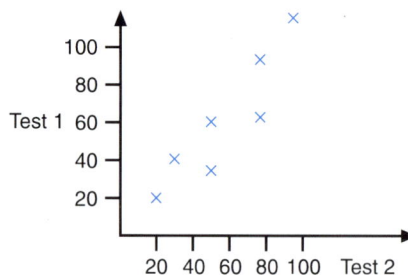

3 The length of the roots of some plants is recorded in the table below.

| Length (cm) | Frequency | Midpoint (x) | Cumulative frequency |
|---|---|---|---|
| $0 \leq L < 5$ | 6 | | |
| $5 \leq L < 10$ | 9 | | |
| $10 \leq L < 15$ | 15 | | |
| $15 \leq L < 20$ | 9 | | |
| $20 \leq L < 25$ | 6 | | |
| $25 \leq L < 30$ | 2 | | |

(a) Find an estimate for the mean length.

(b) What is the modal class?

(c) Draw a cumulative frequency graph. Use scales of 1 cm to 10 on the cumulative frequency axis, and 1 cm to 5 cm on the length axis.

(d) Find the median length.

(e) Find the interquartile range.

# Estimating and calculating the probabilities of events

## Probability

**Probability** is the chance or likelihood that something will happen.

Probabilities must be written as a **fraction**, **decimal** or **percentage**.

All probabilities lie between 0 and 1.

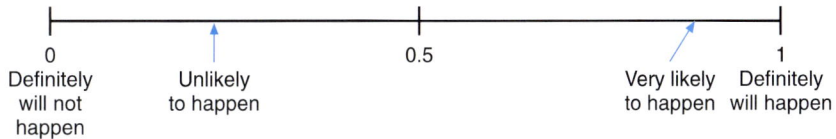

| | | | |
|---|---|---|---|
| 0 | | 0.5 | 1 |
| Definitely will not happen | Unlikely to happen | | Very likely to happen   Definitely will happen |

**Exhaustive events** account for all possible outcomes. For example, the list HH, HT, TH, TT gives all possible outcomes when two coins are thrown together.

**Mutually exclusive events** are events which cannot happen at the same time.

Two students are chosen at random.

Event A – one student has brown hair
Event B – one student wears glasses
}
These are **not mutually exclusive** because brown-haired students could wear glasses.

$$\text{Probability of an event} = \frac{\text{number of ways an event can happen}}{\text{total number of outcomes}}$$

A shortened way of writing the probability of an event is P(event).

### Example
There are 4 red, 3 green and 2 white beads in a bag. John picks out a bead at random from the bag. What is the probability that he picks:

(a) a red bead,    (b) a green bead,    (c) a yellow bead,    (d) a white bead,
(e) a red, green or white bead?

(a) $P(red) = \frac{4}{9}$    (b) $P(green) = \frac{3}{9}$    (c) $P(yellow) = 0$    (d) $P(white) = \frac{2}{9}$

(e) $P(red, green\ or\ white) = \frac{9}{9} = 1$

All probabilities add up to 1.

## Probability of an event not happening

If two events are mutually exclusive, then
P(event will happen)     = 1 − P(event will not happen) or
P(event will not happen) = 1 − P(event will happen)

### Example
The probability that someone gets flu next winter is 0.42. What is the probability that they do not get flu next winter?

P(not get flu) = 1 − P(get flu)

$$= 1 - 0.42$$

$$= 0.58$$

# Expected number

### Example

If a die is thrown 300 times, approximately how many fives are likely to be obtained?

$P(5) = \frac{1}{6} \times 300 = 50$ fives

A 5 is expected $\frac{1}{6}$ of the time.

Key in your calculator: 1 ÷ 6 × 300 =

Remember a die has 6 sides.
$P(5) = \frac{1}{6}$

### Example

The probability of passing a driving test at the first attempt is 0.65. If there are 200 people taking a test for the first time, how many do you expect to pass the test?

$0.65 \times 200 = 130$ people

# Relative frequencies

Experiments can be used to find out the relative frequencies.

If a die is thrown 180 times it would be expected that about 30 twos would be thrown.

$\frac{1}{6} \times 180 = 30$

### Example

Throw the die 180 times but record the frequency of twos every 30 times.

| Number of throws | Total frequency of twos | Relative frequency |
|---|---|---|
| 30 | 3 | 0.1 |
| 60 | 7 | 0.12 |
| 90 | 16 | 0.18 |
| 120 | 19 | 0.16 |
| 150 | 24 | 0.16 |
| 180 | 31 | 0.17 |

This value is obtained by dividing the total frequency of twos by the number of throws, i.e. $\frac{16}{90}$

Drawing a graph shows:

• It is expected that $\frac{1}{6} = 0.16\dot{6} = 0.17$ of the throws will be twos.

• As the number of throws increase, the relative frequency gets closer to the expected probability.

Relative frequency is used as an estimate of probability.

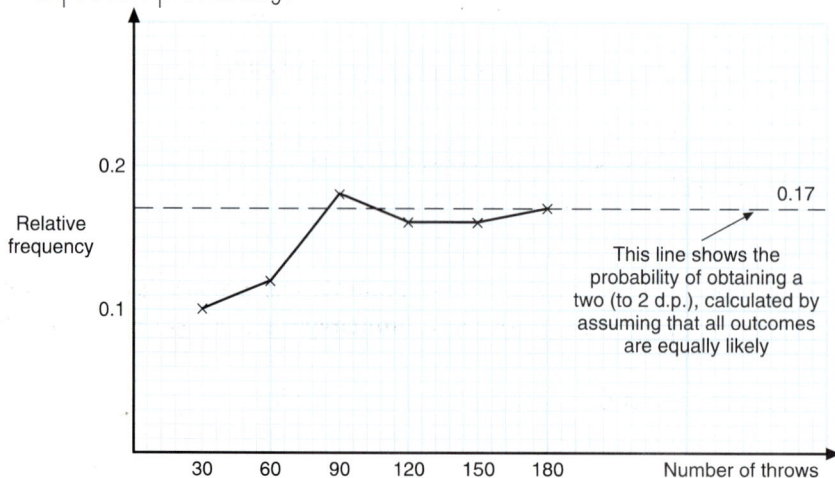

This line shows the probability of obtaining a two (to 2 d.p.), calculated by assuming that all outcomes are equally likely

Relative frequency of an event = $\dfrac{\text{number of times event occurred}}{\text{total number of trials}}$

### Example

When a die was thrown 80 times a six came up 12 times. What is the relative frequency of getting a six?

Number of trials = 80          Relative frequency = $\frac{12}{80}$ = 0.15

Number of sixes = 12

Relative frequency can be used as an estimate of probability. If it is not possible to calculate probability, an experiment is used to find the relative frequency.

# The addition law

If two or more events are **mutually exclusive**, the probability of A or B or C . . . happening is found by **adding** the probabilities. .

P(A or B or C . . .) = P(A) + P(B) + P(C) + . . .

### Example

There are 20 counters in a bag. 6 of these are red and 5 of these are white. Gill picks a counter at random. Find the probability that Gill's counter is either red or white.

P(red) = 6

P(white) = 5

P(red or white) = P(red) + P(white)

Use a fraction key to help you if possible.

$= \frac{6}{20} + \frac{5}{20} = \frac{11}{20}$          'Red' and 'white' are mutually exclusive.

# Independent events

This is when the outcome of the second event is not affected by the outcome of the first.

### Example

Event 1 – the dancer finishes the performance.

Event 2 – I eat sweets during the performance.

# The multiplication law

If two or more events are **independent**, the probability of A and B and C . . . happening together is found by **multiplying** the separate probabilities.

P(A and B and C . . .) = P(A) × P(B) × P(C) . . .

### Example

The probability it will be windy on any day in August is $\frac{3}{10}$. Find the probability that:

(a) it will be windy on both August 1st and August 3rd;

(b) it will be windy on August 9th but not on August 20th.

P(not happening)
= 1 - P(happens)

(a) P(windy **and** windy) = $\frac{3}{10} \times \frac{3}{10} = \frac{9}{100}$

(b) P(windy **and** not windy) = $\frac{3}{10} \times \frac{7}{10} = \frac{21}{100}$

### Example

The probability that Meena does her homework is 0.8. The probability that Jane does her homework is 0.45. Find the probability that both girls do their homework.

P(Meena **and** Jane) = 0.8 × 0.45

= 0.36

## Possible outcomes for two events

A table is helpful when there are outcomes of two events. This kind of table is sometimes known as a **sample space diagram**.

### Example

Two dice are thrown together and their scores are added. Draw a diagram to show all the outcomes. Find the probability of: (a) a score of 7, (b) a score that is a multiple of 3.

To help: put a ring or square around the numbers needed.

There are 36 outcomes.

(a) P(score of 7) = $\frac{6}{36} = \frac{1}{6}$

(b) P(multiple of 3) = $\frac{12}{36} = \frac{1}{3}$

|  |  | First dice | | | | | |
|---|---|---|---|---|---|---|---|
|  |  | 1 | 2 | 3 | 4 | 5 | 6 |
|  | 1 | 2 | ③ | 4 | 5 | ⑥ | 7 |
|  | 2 | ③ | 4 | 5 | ⑥ | 7 | 8 |
| Second dice | 3 | 4 | 5 | ⑥ | 7 | 8 | ⑨ |
|  | 4 | 5 | ⑥ | 7 | 8 | ⑨ | 10 |
|  | 5 | ⑥ | 7 | 8 | ⑨ | 10 | 11 |
|  | 6 | 7 | 8 | ⑨ | 10 | 11 | ⑫ |

## Tree diagrams

These are another way of showing the possible outcomes of two or more events. They may be written horizontally or vertically.

### Example

In a class the probability that a pupil will have their own television is $\frac{5}{7}$, the probability that the pupil will have their own computer is $\frac{1}{4}$.

These events are independent.

Draw a tree diagram of this information.

- Draw the first branch which shows the probabilities of having televisions.
- Put the probabilities on the branches.
- Draw the second branches which show the probabilities of having computers.

| Televisions | Computers | Outcomes |
|---|---|---|

$\frac{5}{7}$ TV

$\frac{1}{4}$ Computer — TV, computer

$\frac{3}{4}$ No computer — TV, no computer

$\frac{2}{7}$ No TV

$\frac{1}{4}$ Computer — No TV, computer

$\frac{3}{4}$ No computer — No TV, no computer

The probabilities on each branch add up to 1.

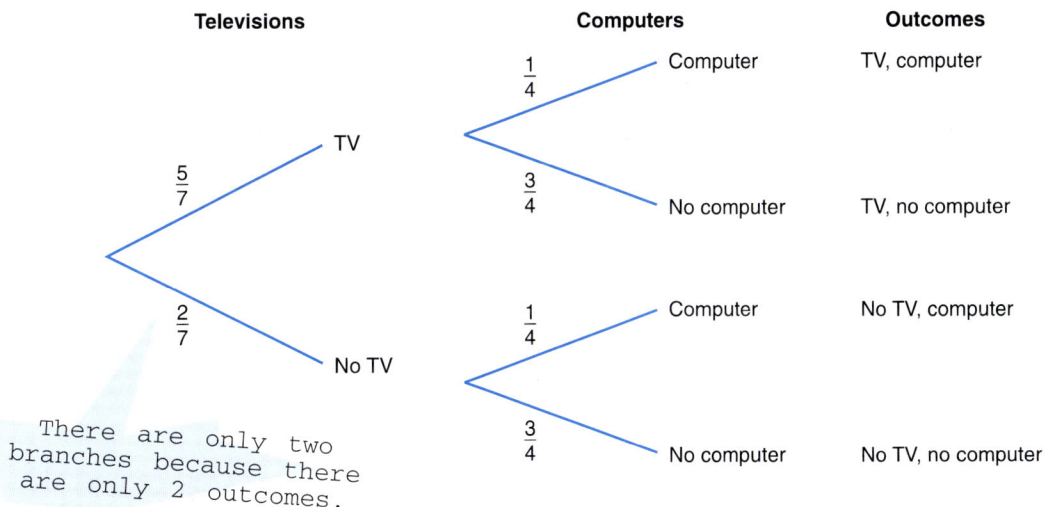

There are only two branches because there are only 2 outcomes.

(a) Find the probability that a pupil will have their own TV and a computer.

$P(\text{TV and computer}) = P(\text{TV}) \times P(\text{computer})$

$= \frac{5}{7} \times \frac{1}{4}$

$= \frac{5}{28}$

Remember P(A and B) = P(A) × P(B)

(b) Find the probability that a pupil will have only 1 of the items.

$P(\text{TV and no computer}) = P(\text{TV}) \times P(\text{no computer})$

$= \frac{5}{7} \times \frac{3}{4}$

$= \frac{15}{28}$

OR

$P(\text{no TV and computer}) = P(\text{no TV}) \times P(\text{computer})$

$= \frac{2}{7} \times \frac{1}{4}$

$= \frac{2}{28}$

Remember P(A or B) = P(A) + P(B)

$P(\text{only one of the items}) = \frac{15}{28} + \frac{2}{28} = \frac{17}{28}$

Use the fraction key on your calculator to work these questions out.

# Estimating and calculating the probabilities of events

## Questions

1  Give an example of two events which are mutually exclusive.

2  Give an example of two events which are independent.

3  The spinner is spun once.

   What is the probability that the spinner lands on:

   (a)  a number 1, (b) an odd number, (c) a multiple of 3?

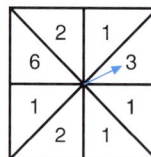

4  The probability the bus is late is $\frac{7}{9}$. What is the probability it is not late?

5  The probability of getting a C grade in maths is 0.48. If 300 people sit the exam, how many are expected to get a C?

6  When a die was thrown 320 times, a three came up 62 times. What is the relative frequency of getting a three?

7  A die is thrown. What is the probability of scoring a 4 or an odd number?

8  The probability that Emma is late for school is 0.3. The probability that Mark is late for school is 0.4. What is the probability they are both late?

9  Two dice are thrown together and their totals added.

   (a)  Fill in the table.

   (b)  What is the probability that:

      (i)  the total score is 7,

      (ii) the total score is odd?

| | | Dice 1 | | | | |
|---|---|---|---|---|---|---|
| | 1 | 2 | 3 | 4 | 5 | 6 |
| 1 | | | | | | |
| 2 | | | | | | |
| Dice 2  3 | | | | | | |
| 4 | | | | | | |
| 5 | | | | | | |
| 6 | | | | | | |

10 Moira and Robi play a game of darts and a game of snooker.

   The probability Moira wins darts is 0.7.

   The probability Robi wins snooker is 0.6.

   (a)  Complete the tree diagram.

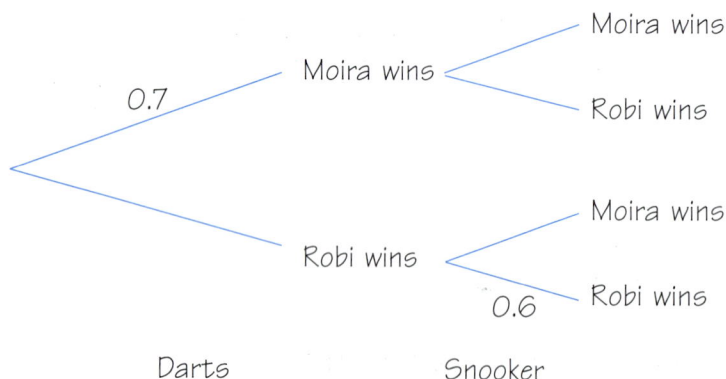

   (b)  Calculate the probability that Moira wins both games.

   (c)  Calculate the probability that they win one game each.

# Answers

## Place value and the number system

1  3 °C

2  (a) 4        (b) −16      (c) −12      (d) −12      (e) 5        (f) 6

3  (a) 6.25     (b) 18.07    (c) 106.28   (d) 3.76     (e) 27.06    (f) 18.09

4  (a) 0.003 79           (b) 27 500             (c) 307 000

5  $0.\dot{6}$, $66.\dot{6}\%$

6  0.274, $\frac{4}{7}$, 61%, $\frac{9}{10}$, 0.93, 94%

7  (a) $12^{12}$    (b) $9^{-6}$    (c) 1    (d) $18^{8}$    (e) $4^{10}$    (f) 1

8  (a) $6.94 \times 10^{8}$    (b) $3.729 \times 10^{-3}$    (c) $2.79 \times 10^{3}$    (d) $2.7 \times 10^{-2}$

9  (a) $4.35 \times 10^{10}$    (b) $4.59 \times 10^{16}$

10
| Fraction | Decimal | Percentage |
|----------|---------|------------|
| $\frac{3}{4}$ | 0.75 | 75% |
| $\frac{2}{5}$ | 0.4 | 40% |
| $\frac{1}{3}$ | $0.\dot{3}$ | $33.\dot{3}\%$ |

## Relationships between numbers and computation methods

1  2, 3, 5, 7, 11, 13, 17, 19

2  HCF: 12;    LCM: 120

3  (a) ±8              (b) 6

4  (a) $\frac{12}{9}$           (b) $\frac{p}{x}$

5  (a) 2620          (b) 240 000       (c) 1240

   (d) 0.008         (e) 5             (f) 0.126

   (g) 120           (h) 7000          (i) 20 000

6  (a) $\frac{1}{3}$        (b) $\frac{7}{20}$        (c) $\frac{6}{13}$        (d) $\frac{16}{27}$

7  74.6% (to 1 d.p.)

8  247 mm

9  9.9 lb

10 £68 068 (to nearest £1)

11 £411.76 (to nearest 1p)

12 36 cm

13 (a) 14.45 (to 2 d.p.)    (b) 769.6 (to 1 d.p.)

14 $\dfrac{30^{2} + 100}{2 \times 5} = 100$

15 £113.40

16 27

# Solving numerical problems

1  £7186.62
2  (a)  £3524.25        (b)  £13 827.75
3  2.25 m.p.h.
4  8.57 hours (or 8 hours 34 minutes)
5  2.2̇ g/cm$^3$
6  (a)  £1800          (b)  £6180
7  Super Sid's; £33.33
8  (a)  706 500 lire   (b)  £60.03

# Functional relationships

1  (a)  20.4          (b)  29.82          (c)  20.736          (d)  4.60
2  (a)  $U_n = 4n + 1$   (b)  $U_n = n^2 + 2$
3

|            | (a) | (b) | (c) |
|------------|-----|-----|-----|
| Gradient   | 4   | −2  | 2   |
| Intercept  | −1  | 3   | 4   |

4  (a)  66.6̇ m.p.h.    (b)  1 hour
   (c)  50 m.p.h.      (d)  About 1442
5  (a)

| $x$ | −3  | −2 | −1 | 0 | 1 | 2  | 3  |
|-----|-----|----|----|---|---|----|----|
| $y$ | −24 | −5 | 2  | 3 | 4 | 11 | 30 |

   (b)  Check the graph (below).
   (c)  When $y = 15$, $x = 2.3$ (to 1 d.p.)

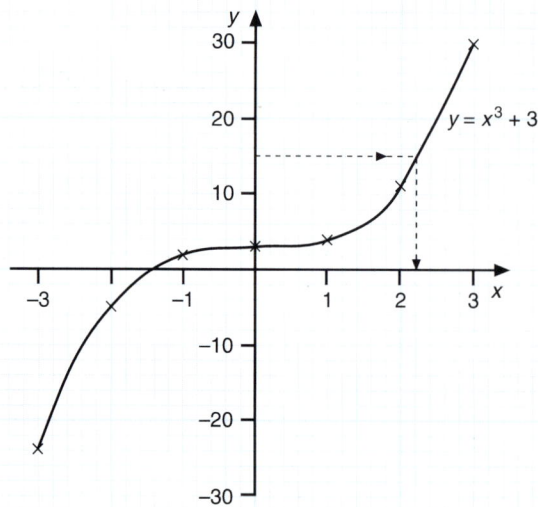

$y = x^3 + 3$

6  Graph A = c        Graph B = f        Graph C = d        Graph D = e

# Equations and formulae

1  (a) $20x^5$         (b) $3x^4$              (c) $16x^6$              (d) 1
2  (a) $3x^2 - 4x - 12$  (b) $x^2 + 4x - 12$   (c) $x^2 - 12x + 36$   (d) $6x^2 - 4x + 3xy - 2y$
3  (a) $q(p + r)$       (b) $5x^2(1 + 2xy)$    (c) $(x - 1)(x - 4)$    (d) $(x + 8)(x - 8)$
4  (a) $a = \dfrac{r}{5}$    (b) $a = \dfrac{r^2 - b}{4}$    (c) $a = 2q - \tfrac{1}{2}r$ or $\dfrac{4q - r}{2}$

**5** (a) $x = 3$      (b) $x = 1.5$      (c) $x = 1$      (d) $x = 50$

**6** $a = 2, b = -1$

**7** (a) $x = 0$ or $x = 7$      (b) $x = 4$ or $x = 5$

**8** (a) $x \le \frac{10}{3}$ or $x \le 3.\dot{3}$      (b) $1 < x \le 8$

# Shape, space and measures
## Properties of shapes

**1** Octagon

**2** Check drawings of cube, cuboid, sphere, cylinder, cone, triangular prism, square-based pyramid and triangular-based pyramid (tetrahedron). (See page 50.)

**3**

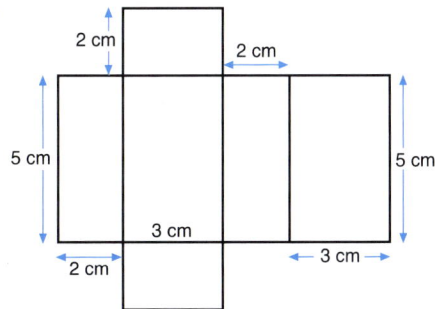

**4** (a) $a = 150°$      (b) $b = 70°, c = 110°, d = 70°$
    (c) $a = 50°, b = 50°, c = 50°, d = 130°$

**5** (a) $72°$      (b) $108°$

**6** (a) $17.2$ cm      (b) $20.0$ cm

**7** (a) $20$ cm      (b) $68.0$ cm      (c) $17.1°$

# Properties of position, movement and transformation

**1** The interior angle of a heptagon is $128.6°$. Two heptagons together will leave a gap of $102.9°$. Hence they do not tessellate.

**2** (a) $060°$      (b) $340°$

**3** 2 to the left, 3 upwards

**4**

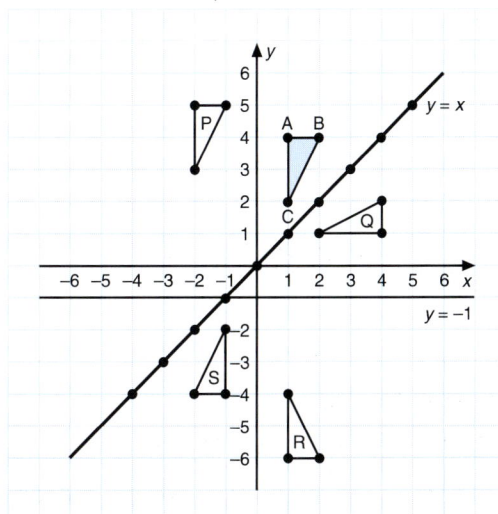

5

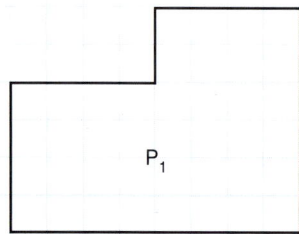

6

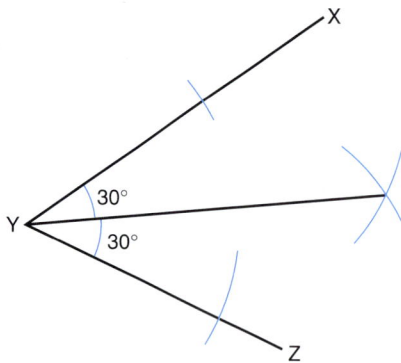

7  (a)  7.7 cm (3 s.f.)          (b)  9.12 cm (3 s.f.)

## Measures

1  3.5 kg
2  42 lb
3  $10\frac{1}{2}$ pints
4  $9.15 \leq 9.2 < 9.25$
5  (a)  68.0 cm² (3 s.f.)          (b)  63.6 cm² (3 s.f.)
   (c)  63.6 cm² (3 s.f.)          (d)  208 cm² (3 s.f.)
6  (a)  1750 cm³ (3 s.f.)          (b)  601 cm³ (3 s.f.)
7  20.3 cm (3 s.f.)
8  (a)  perimeter       (b)  volume       (c)  volume       (d)  area

## Handling data

## Processing and interpreting data

1  (a)

| Height (cm) | Frequency |
| --- | --- |
| $140 \leq h < 145$ | 6 |
| $145 \leq h < 150$ | 10 |
| $150 \leq h < 155$ | 11 |
| $155 \leq h < 160$ | 5 |
| $160 \leq h < 165$ | 2 |

   (b)  34

(c)

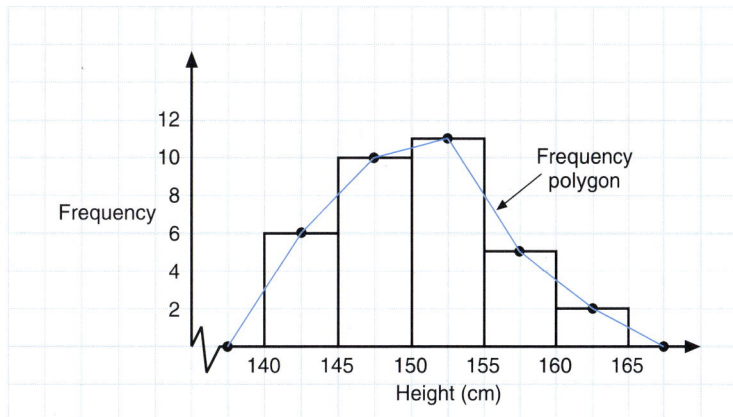

2 (a) Positive correlation – the better you did in test 1, the better you did in test 2.

(b)

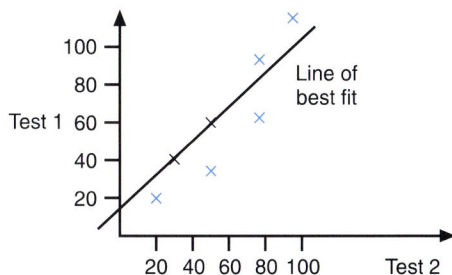

3

| Length (cm) | Frequency | Midpoint (x) | Cumulative frequency |
|---|---|---|---|
| $0 \leq L < 5$ | 6 | 2.5 | 6 |
| $5 \leq L < 10$ | 9 | 7.5 | 15 |
| $10 \leq L < 15$ | 15 | 12.5 | 30 |
| $15 \leq L < 20$ | 9 | 17.5 | 39 |
| $20 \leq L < 25$ | 6 | 22.5 | 45 |
| $25 \leq L < 30$ | 2 | 27.5 | 47 |

(a) mean: 13.1 cm (3 s.f.)

(b) modal class: $10 \leq L < 15$

(c)

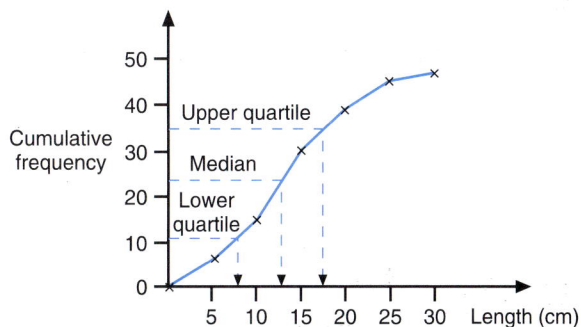

(d) median: about 12.8 cm

(e) interquartile range: about 9.7 cm

# Estimating and calculating the probabilities of events

1 Event 1 – you get a head when you throw a coin.

Event 2 – you get a tail when you throw a coin.

2 Throwing two coins together.

3 (a) $\frac{4}{8} = \frac{1}{2}$    (b) $\frac{5}{8}$    (c) $\frac{2}{8} = \frac{1}{4}$

4 $\frac{2}{9}$

5 144

6 $\frac{62}{320} = \frac{31}{160} = 0.19$ (2 d.p.)

7 $\frac{2}{3}$

8 0.12

9 (a)

|  | Dice 1 |  |  |  |  |  |
|---|---|---|---|---|---|---|
|  | 1 | 2 | 3 | 4 | 5 | 6 |
| **1** | 2 | 3 | 4 | 5 | 6 | 7 |
| **2** | 3 | 4 | 5 | 6 | 7 | 8 |
| Dice 2 **3** | 4 | 5 | 6 | 7 | 8 | 9 |
| **4** | 5 | 6 | 7 | 8 | 9 | 10 |
| **5** | 6 | 7 | 8 | 9 | 10 | 11 |
| **6** | 7 | 8 | 9 | 10 | 11 | 12 |

(b) (i) $\frac{6}{36} = \frac{1}{6}$  (ii) $\frac{18}{36} = \frac{1}{2}$

10 (a)

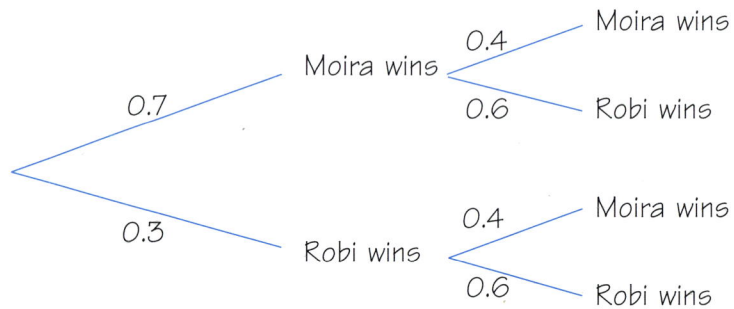

(b) 0.28

(c) 0.54